DEEPENING OUR CONNECTION
A GUIDE FOR THE WISDOM YEARS

Darrienne Stuart Heller

Original Art by Darrienne Stuart Heller
Book cover design by Derek Rickles

ISBN: 1490928200
ISBN-13: 9781490928203

I watch the words spill across these pages
wanting to connect
with the shining presence that waits
in that silent space where we truly meet
beyond the hub bub of the restless mind.
Darrienne

CONTENTS

ACKNOWLEDGMENTS
PREFACE (Indra's Net}
INTRODUCTION

PART ONE
WELCOME TO THE ANGEL OHANA
Overview and Purpose

PART TWO
THE GUIDE
Purpose of The Guide

PART THREE
HOW TO USE THE GUIDE

PART FOUR
HOW TO BEGIN AN ANGEL OHANA

PART FIVE
THEMES AND GUIDELINES FOR
THE MEETINGS

PART SIX
DEEPENING OUR SUPPORT

PART SEVEN
DEEPENING OUR CONNECTION

PART EIGHT
GUIDELINES FOR FACILITATORS

EPILOGUE

ACKNOWLEDGMENTS

Na'u ka hau'oli
It is my happiness to share this with you.

My gratitude goes to all the Angels in our 'Ohana for this book and The Guide within. With your commitment and the courage to take a chance on birthing The Angel 'Ohana these groups now stand on their own.

To my beloved friends Lili Townsend, David "Ilili" Kapralic, Lotus Dancer, Helen Kritzler, Myrna Stone, Summer Richardson, Judith Small, Kranto, Patricia Hendricks, River Penner and Pat Schulte who were the wind under my wings as this book became a reality.

I give special thanks to Stephen and Ondrea Levine who share their wisdom through the books *A Year to Live* and *Who Dies.*

As always I'm grateful for my constant 'love teachers'....my children Nicolette, Rick and Derek and my grandkids River and Lukas.

PREFACE

The spirit of this book was a seed of inspiration planted in me long ago by my mother. The story of Indra's net was the seed that grew into the realization that all life everywhere is connected. I was comforted to know I was not alone and belonged to something greater than I could imagine.

INDRA'S NET

Far away in the heavenly abode of the great god Indra, there is a wonderful net that is hung in such a way that it stretches out in all directions. There is a single glittering jewel at the net's every node, and since that net is infinite the jewels are infinite as well. The jewels shine like stars, a wonderful sight to behold. If we look closely at each jewel, we will discover that in its polished surface there are reflected all the other jewels in the infinite net. Not only that, each jewel reflected in this one jewel is also reflected in all the other jewels. When you look as far as you can see and then beyond you know all is infinitely connected.

It's inspiring to know our tiny lives are powerful
in the larger scheme of things.
What we do makes a difference and our choices carry an affect.

The ultimate challenge before the world today is to find ways to live as one interrelated whole. We have brought ourselves to the precipice where the old ways of survival must give way. Simple to see, challenging to change from old strategies of "survival of the fittest" to survival of the most caring.

There is a longing, an innate passion in the collective heart of humanity to connect. You can see increasing attempts in shopping malls with cell phones and with social media such as Face Book and Twitter with new ideas popping up every day. The attempt doesn't satisfy for we aren't truly meeting eye-to-eye and heart to heart. We miss the mark because we have lost our way in the entanglement of technology. There is memory in our DNA of tribal living, family like groups such as Kibbutzim in Israel and the 'ohanas of Hawaii.

After years of living increasingly separate lives in a divided society and friends and family spread across the world we remember and envision a life as one connected whole. We naturally want to deepen our connection when we realize we are already connected. We always have been at one with and affected by all there is from the tiniest frog in the rainforest to supernovas and our nurturing planet. It is said, "The truth will set you free." We have gone against this truth and see we have been set off on illusions of separation from each other and our true nature. Looking deeply within yourself and others you may see a pattern of movement toward more true connection. People are beginning to shift from isolated lives into neighborhoods and communities. Churches and gatherings are full of people wanting to be together as friends. The inherent need to give and receive support asks for our attention. This is the time for social connection to become heartfelt with those who care and rebuild our trust in each other and all living things.

In the visuals of Indra's Net we see each of us as a shining jewel reflecting every other jewel. As the wisdom of the ancients filters down through the ages into the minds of the present, this image becomes more than a metaphor in The Angel 'Ohana. In Hawaiian culture, 'ohana means an extended family with the intention of mutual support and affection. Family and friends are bound together and members cooperate and remember one another. Unrelated people come together as one, an intentional family chosen to make a better life.

As we gather in these special groups it is evident that everyone makes a difference and the whole affects each one. As the human story begins to change from "me to we" The Angel 'Ohana provides a proving ground. Being on the leading edge of a wave to create a better future the later years become a meaningful adventure.

If this resonates with you at this time of your life, welcome to The Angel 'Ohana.

INTRODUCTION

There will come a time when you believe everything is finished.
That will be the beginning.
Louis L'more

Are you a baby boomer, someone in the midst of the later years of life or a person of any age with your own flavor of transitions? Are you wondering what these years have to offer and how to navigate the challenges? The powerful phases of human life can be uplifting and illuminating with a different approach to the unexpected aspects of any age.

This book is about The Angel 'Ohana, who we are and what we do. These specially designed support groups are based on the premise that life is too difficult to live alone. The capacity to realize our happiness is intrinsically wrapped up with others to realize their own.

The book is also a guide to support those who want to form an Angel 'Ohana with others in their community. The Guide can benefit individuals, couples and families and groups already created for other reasons. Our groups bring people together as a family of friends who care about and support each other in all phases of life. This is not the usual support group. We *learn* to give and receive support in all its many facets. In our wisdom we know it's time to discover what these years have to teach, embrace our mortality and deepen our connection with each other and all life. Ultimately the journey we take in The Angel 'Ohana as in life is about awakening into Spirit and deepening into love.

The book is a way to share what I've learned, the fruition of my wisdom years. There are times when I offer my experiences with The Angel 'Ohana and lessons of life. Your group will give you the same opportunity to share with others what life is teaching you. Questions relative to each theme call forth a deeper knowing than opinions and beliefs. *In this way we find our true voice and discover our own wisdom.*

As a member of these special 'ohanas you are an integral part of developing an interrelated way of life. In these days of personal and planetary separateness there is a hunger for ways to realize and live our natural connection. The single most cause of stress and dis-ease is isolation. Isolation kills, community heals. We are meant to support each other.

The first group started on the island of Maui in 2004. Everyone realized our group was truly an 'ohana. What about the angels? I see an angel within each of us who knows us well, who guides and teaches us and wants the best for us. In the 'family of angels' these qualities are shared and become a part of our everyday lives.

In earlier days The Angel 'Ohana was for women only. Times have changed and since these groups create their own destiny, men are welcome. The groups can be men only, women only or women and men together. I use "she" and "her" when writing about both men and women.

This century is a turning point for men and women to co-create the art of mutual empowerment. Those of us in our later years are perfect for the job. Our wisdom years are the perfect time to mine a wealth of experience in support of our sisters and brothers of any age. Men and women are teachers and guides for each other as we have been since the beginning of humanity. May The Angel 'Ohana be an arena for realizing these self-evident truths.

The guide is designed with the purpose of supporting individuals who want to form an Angel 'Ohana. The format for meetings is easy to follow. The content offers seasoned guidelines from my years with these groups. A Guideline for Facilitators provides a manual to support facilitation of the meetings. Ways to enhance our later years of deepening are woven into the content as threads are woven into tapestry. Each member plays a part in creating this work of art that is always in the process of becoming a deep and abiding family of friends.

How it all began:

Something happened when I wasn't looking. My changing body gave me the first clue. Print was shrinking, my hair was thinning and my waist was thickening. Oh no, could this be that dreaded event called "aging"? Since our youth oriented mindset can't prepare for what it denies, I was on my own and in shock. Aging! Now, there's a loaded word that can explode into a million misconceptions.

I asked myself, "Is something wrong with my body, with me, and the whole experience of these later years? Will I become discarded in our throwaway culture? Do I have to accept this fate alone and helpless?"

Now, all those anti-aging ads began to make sense. They seemed to be rushing to my side with anti-aging ammunition. However, the more I tried to patch up what's left of fleeting youth, the older I felt. The pricey Band-Aids weren't working. I didn't need my glasses to see this is a losing battle. I would have to find another way to regain my confidence. If what I was looking for wasn't out there with the anti-aging pros, I'd look to myself for guidance. I would discover what these years are really about and see what was taking place beyond the wrinkles on my face.

What I thought was a catastrophe was waking me up to a new life filled with opportunities unavailable in my youth. I was off on an adventure into the unknown where anything and everything could happen. My pile of years no longer pulled me down. They were my launching pad.

I turned to my friends, whose lives were also whirlwinds of change. We felt like Dorothy in the Wizard of Oz. We knew we weren't in Kansas any more and wanted to find our way back. There was much to learn for there was a bumpy road ahead. This could be a real life adventure or a slippery slide into myopia.

Our families and friends were an emotional or physical distance apart. Many of us were on our own due to divorce, being widows or just wanting our independence. At this time of our lives we needed a new family, a "family of friends".

My friends and I gathered to pool our resources and hard earned wisdom to explore the later years. We had few models or teachers so we became teachers and guides for each other. The insights we shared let us know these are truly the wisdom years.

Since I had been trained at UCLA to design and facilitate groups, I put together a format for everyone to participate. The Guide is what developed in the hands and hearts of the growing circles of the Angel 'Ohana. As we learned what friendship really means we knew without a doubt we were not alone. We became our name, a true 'ohana and a family of angels.

In our youth oriented culture have the later years been overlooked? Nature is wise. She gives us a gift of time to develop a wiser more compassionate way of life. Due to science and technology we live in a world our ancestors never knew. What will we do with our still vibrant lives now that 60 is the new 40 and 70 is the new 50? This is our challenge, a right of passage into a new paradigm and our legacy for others who follow. In The Angel 'Ohana we embrace the challenge and receive the gift of our wisdom years to make these the best years of all.

What is done anywhere is done everywhere and each of us plays our part.

PART ONE

WELCOME TO THE ANGEL 'OHANA
Overview and Purpose

Blessed is the influence of one true, loving human soul on another.
George Elliot

"We don't set out to save the world; we set out to wonder how other people are doing and to reflect on how our actions affect other people's hearts."
Pema Chodron

The gift of the second part of life needs to be treated with care and used wisely. Are we missing the true benefit of this unique time of life when we struggle on our own and feel alone.

The Angel 'Ohana offers a new perspective in the realm of personal growth. Books and teachers give us wise philosophies and valuable concepts about how to meet life's challenges gracefully and intelligently. Research tells us healthy longevity comes from companionship and life long learning. Psychologist say people who engage in deep conversation and spend less time in small talk are happier. A safe place to give and receive strengthens the heart. Spiritual connection plays an integral part in finding purpose and peace of mind. *The Angel 'Ohana provides a way to make these ideals and suggestions a living experience.*

Themes in the guide evolve from natural events our culture chooses to ignore such as aging, illness and our own mortality. These human milestones are what Siddhartha's father tried to hide to protect his son from life's realities. Like the young Buddha in the making, we discover the *whole of life* is where wisdom is born and compassion has its roots,

I will not tell you it's easy. These groups will call upon everything you've learned and what you have yet to learn. One must be committed to see and do what it takes to build trust and learn team support in order to become a true 'ohana. Embracing our differences takes patience and trusting the process of bonding. I *will* tell you it's inspiring to be a part of creating a 'new kind of family' of life-long friends. No one knows what the years may bring. Not to worry, for the inclination to connect and care for each other is our true nature.

The following was offered in the sharing circle as members were discussing the qualities of a true 'ohana. "To be in an 'ohana family means that we commit to stay together no matter what happens. If we have conflict within the family we can trust each other enough to stay together and not leave the family. We hang together knowing we will grow and become stronger through challenging times."

The Purposes of the Angel 'Ohana

The following is a variety of purposes in the Angel 'Ohana. You may discover more for this journey is as unique as you are. Our journey *together* becomes a co-creation of purpose with surprises for all as we fulfill the potential of these groups.

- **Creating Our Connection:** Ancient teachings, early cultures and now the World Wide Web show us we are one planetary community interwoven with all life at all times. In The Angel Ohana we aspire to realize and deepen this connection.

- **Forming a Family of Friends:** The word family has many meanings. This is a family of a different hue. We start out together and create our own family from 'scratch'. Some ingredients are 'circles of sharing and listening' and including our differences with respect.
- **Sharing Commitment:** Commitment means we can count on each other to truly be there and care. Knowing that is a big relief that warms the heart and calms the mind.
- **Providing Support:** Mutual support has many facets. Getting to know the various ways of giving and receiving is a dance to discover.
- **Learning from Each Other:** We have found our teachers and they are us.
- **Aging Without Getting Old:** Social connection is a common thread of healthy longevity. Change and challenge is a recipe for adventure. Gratitude is a fountain of youth. In essence we are ageless. You aren't getting old; it's the body that ages.
- **Deepening Our Connection:** The later years are a perfect time to remember who we are and what we have always been. Growing older with a family of angels by our side makes all the difference now and when the time comes to leave our body.
- **Embracing Our Mortality:** When we embrace impermanence and our mortality we can embrace life.
- **Experiencing Trust and Vulnerability:** Deep connection goes beyond the exterior where we can truly meet. Vulnerability is the key that only opens in safety. Trust resides within us all when given a chance. This is our opportunity.
- **Co-creating Our Bonds:** The very act of co-creating our groups bonds us in a shared experience of pure joy.

- **Living Our Gratitude:** The grace in gratitude kisses the weight of the world goodbye and fills our hearts with happiness. As the years go by simply being together deepens our gratefulness.
- **Sharing Our Love:** Love is realizing we *are* the love we seek. Sharing this love deepens our connection.

It is my happiness to share The Angel 'Ohana with you.

PART TWO

THE GUIDE

The Real Work
It may be that when we no longer know what to do
we have come to our real work,
and that when we no longer know which way to go
we have come to our real journey.
The mind that is not baffled is not employed
The impeded stream is the one that sings.
Wendell Berry

The guide offers a variety ways to make it possible to co-create a family of friends with the intention of mutual support and affection. This transition from cultural admiration of individual accomplishments to building mutual trust and group bonding is a challenge. The process can *'baffle the mind'.* Could this be the *'impeded stream'* that sings with a promise of 'ohana?

When I entered my later years, a turning point in body, mind and spirit, I knew I wanted to enjoy this next phase of life. Satisfying my longing for community built on trust and support was essential. As in most transitions I had one foot in the past and the other *no longer knowing what to do or which way to go.* This time is always a sort of limbo then something new begins to open, first a tiny bud then a full blossoming of what's next.

Frequently we don't allow others into our lives when we need them the most. Often we don't take the time or have forgotten how to develop intimate and lasting relationships. In our wisdom years we realize the importance of building trust that offers the safety to truly meet another beyond the exterior. These are the friends that will be at our side when its time to leave our body.

In my years with the Angel 'Ohana I realized my *real work* and perhaps you will too. The "work" of becoming true and abiding friends has made it possible to *embrace* my later years in a culture that resists aging and all that follows. This was well said by one of the elder angels as she was approaching her nineties:
"What happens in life doesn't matter, no matter what you think. It's the people along the way that are important. Now I'm content and complete. It's wonderful to feel this way at this time of my life. You have to be prepared for it and that's what The Angel 'Ohana does."

THE PURPOSE of THE Guide

The purpose of the guide is to offer:

- **Support** for those who want to form an Angel 'Ohana.
- **Guidance** for navigating the uncharted waters of the wisdom years.
- **Group consciousness** allowing each of us to flourish within one interrelated whole.
- **Self-expression**, vital to the co-creative work of creating a new kind of family.
- **Structure** providing safety for groups to naturally evolve instead of being a product of preconception.
- **Inquiry** that can open to our "real work" and our "real journey". "What you're looking for is doing the looking."
- **Themes and questions** as a source for shared exploration and discovery.
- **Vision** so people worldwide can form a family of friends.

The themes begin with the topics of healthy aging and matters relative to our later years. What naturally follows is contemplating our own mortality. Embracing death and dying can open us to the magnificent gift of being alive.

Topics in the guide are formed around four themes:
- The Later Years, an Adventure of a Lifetime
- Embracing Our Mortality
- Deepening Our Support
- Deepening Our Connection, a co-creation by group members

Giving and receiving support is an opportunity to offer our compassion and realize the truth of our limitations. This is a work in progress and always changing depending on the person and each situation. Support can mean simply listening or attending to a person in crisis. Sharing the caring and team support allow friendships to flourish without compassion burnout. Giving and receiving support can be one of the most creative and intimate group experiences.

Questions in each theme are an essential part of The Angel Ohana When members respond to the questions in each topic we can learn from each other. These questions are designed to reveal our often-unacknowledged wisdom. As we look beneath the surface of our lives we often surprise ourselves with our own intuitive knowing. In this way we learn to trust ourselves and so does everyone else.

Learning from each other is the strength of our groups. Themes and questions in each topic call for a deeper inquiry than casual conversation. There are no right or wrong answers and often no answers at all leaving an open mind.

Loving Kindness for our selves and each other
I encourage members to show compassion for each other. At times the sharing can touch places in ourselves that are vulnerable and need a loving response. Being heard in the circle is often enough. A caring hug or words of understanding can be given at a break or

after the meeting. It may be appropriate to ask a member at the time of sharing if there is a group request for support. (This is not done often in order to honor everyone's time to share.)

The format is simple and easy to follow. Our meetings take place in a circle of sharing and listening where a common field evolves. Each member can share without comment, advice or interruption. In this way the group becomes a safe haven where trust can grow, a cherished achievement in our society.

The content of the themes offers a shared journey through our later years and the grace of blossoming into our wisdom years.

The foundation of The Angel 'Ohana is trust.
The inspiration is deepening our connection.
The heart and soul is support.

This is how we become a family of friends...... for life.

PART THREE

HOW TO USE THE GUIDE

Individuals, couples and families with children and grand parents can benefit from using the guide. Just tailor the format and processes to suit your situation.
Couples and family members can use the guide as a small group including Guidelines for Facilitators. The purpose is the same for individuals as it is for groups. Inquiry is interaction with oneself in a group or on one's own.

If you choose to explore the themes and questions on your own I suggest writing down your responses in a workbook. Seeing your responses in writing and noticing what changes with time fosters awareness. Be sure to respond to questions of your own as they arise. Remember there are no right or wrong answers. Questions are pointers to deeper observation. In this way inquiry becomes a journey of discovery. After this experience you may choose to organize a group. Group bonding offers support and a feeling of "family".

How do I know this is true? I look inside myself and see.
Lao-tzu

There is no one person, book or teacher outside of yourself that can tell you what is most important to you or how to live your life. The guide can be a resource that points the way to your own inner guidance. When we share what's true for us it often resonates with what's true for others. In this way we become teachers and guides for each other and our friendship deepens.

The guide provides a never-ending learning experience and a manual for the wisdom years. Let's make sure we use these later years well. Surely it's not a time to fall by the way side. It is a time to take inventory of our wisdom years and share our life of experience.

We Are Teachers and Guides for Each Other

"When the student is ready, the teacher will appear."
Buddhist Proverb

There are few places in our society where the voices of elders are heard and appreciated. Our meetings are circles of exchange to harvest the experience of a lifetime. Wisdom comes to life as we respond to the topics and questions that invite a deeper inquiry than casual conversations.

Who could be better teachers and guides to explore our common needs and collective interests? By sharing our challenges and concerns we provide a valuable service to each other. We become a team to investigate the most effective means of navigating all the new unknowns of the later years. Together we are a resource for a life of learning for years to come.

Building Trust and Our Differences

In each group and among members I have seen self-confidence and trust flourish in unison. This is an opportunity to relax and be ourselves. Regardless of what has been shared, or what has been done, acceptance takes the place of the pain of judgment. We begin to see each other in the clear light of trust. Trust encourages even the shyest one of us to take the chance to be our most loveable and loving selves.

Unfortunately, we're embedded in a society that tells us we must be fearful. It is a noble cause to learn another way to live, for ourselves and for all humanity. When we let down our walls of protection we can finally "see" each other beyond all our differences. This is when we can truly meet. The wonder of this "meeting" is simultaneous connection with our selves, with the other and the oneness of all life.

Trust is one of those little words like 'aging' and 'love' that is a tiny door to a vast continent of introspection. Whether it is in regard to individuals, groups, corporations or nations it has many expressions and applications. For example: There is trust in one's own innate goodness and intuitive knowing. Another kind of trust is the confidence that someone's intention is not to harm. There is faith in God, or Nature, or the Universe, or your own personal Source. One of Einstein's most provocative questions was, "Is the Universe benign?" Can we trust that the true nature of life is harmless? In essence at the core of each living thing are actions meant to do no harm? This is a good topic for inquiry.

Some Key Elements for Building Trust:
With our intention to be friends for life we explore what is needed for this ideal to become a reality. With the intention of building trust there are many challenges. When we respond to the need to feel connected we begin our journey to trust our selves and each other.

- Trust in Our Selves.
    Learning to trust our selves is the first step to trusting others. Knowing ourselves without a critical mind or fabrications is the beginning of self-trust.

Learning who we can trust and who we don't trust soon follows. Both self-trust and trust in others requires letting go of critical judgment.

- Allowing Time for Trust to Evolve

It takes time to know another beyond surface persona and differences and nurture self-confidence and personal worth. The walls of protection finally relax into the joy of trusting.

- Agreements

Keeping agreements builds trust such as coming to the group on time or letting the contact person know you will be late or are not able to come. These and keeping other agreements lets members know they can count on you.

- Commitment

We are committed to honoring each member of the group and their own mode of self-expression. This means each of us is dedicated to creating a safe environment where we can be our most authentic self thereby becoming the best of who we are.

- Consistent Connection

The longer we know each other our trust becomes stronger. Consistent presence in the meetings deepens our bonds of trust.

- Our Differences Can Teach Trust

Remember how it was when you first lived with someone? No matter how compatible you thought you were after awhile your differences became apparent.

Now What? You can either bolt or stick around to see what can be learned.

When you come together for the first few meetings, it's often assumed that beliefs, ideals and values are mostly the same. As time goes by personal points of view begin to surface. Layers of what seemed to be similarities dissolve to reveal there are times we don't think alike at all.

My Experience With Trust In the Groups
When differences began to occur in the first group judgment soon followed. Those judgments could have catapulted the group into a

great pout. It was the inborn motivation for connection that came to the rescue. With the intention to stay open we learned listening to other's opinions actually broadened our own view. It wasn't necessary to *believe* another's point of view. We simply opened to another way of seeing. Then something amazing happened. We found a person just like ourselves who wanted to be heard and accepted as they are.

PART FOUR

HOW TO BEGIN AN ANGEL 'OHANA

We will rise to the better angel of our nature.
Abraham Lincoln

The Angel 'Ohana is offered without charge. There is no one teacher because every member is a teacher as we unfold into our years of wisdom. I recommend a facilitator in order to keep the group on track, keep the sanctity and safety of sharing and take care of group business.

New groups usually begin when one or two people want to start an Angel 'Ohana. The organizer begins with a few friends and their friends. The group can begin by gathering six or seven people and often grows to nine or ten in the first meetings. I recommend about ten people to keep the group intimate. Eight makes a cozy meeting. Members often want to add a close friend or two when they experience the benefit. Additional members can be decided by group discussion and a unanimous vote.

Reading *Deepening Our Connection* is the best way for potential members to know if the Angel 'Ohana meets their needs. The book can also be beneficial if they don't want to be in a group. The guide can be used as a workbook for couples or families with children and grandparents. Groups already formed for other reasons can also benefit from the purpose and the different format.

As a trailblazer, a way shower for people entering their wisdom years, the purpose and value of the book may inspire you to organize a group.

Introductory Gathering For a New Group

What You Will Need

The book, *Deepening Our Connection* can guide you through the content and format of the meetings. Knowing the overall purpose of the Angel 'Ohana and how to facilitate the group supports members and the facilitator. Reading the book can deepen your experience of themes and topics and enhance your participation in the group.

- **Name, phone numbers, email, address and Birthday of each member.** This list is gathered at the first meeting. The contact person will send a copy by email or make a hard copy for each member. Remember to add new members to the roster.
- **A facilitator** (to start the meetings, keep the group on track and plan for the next meeting) Usually the organizer takes this role for a few meetings. Ask the group if anyone would like to facilitate the meetings. See Guidelines for Facilitators.
- **A contact person** This volunteer makes calls or sends emails to announce meetings or changes and a reminder of the theme for the next meeting. Members let the contact person know if unable to attend a the meeting.
- **An item to hold for sharing** (such as a crystal or heart shaped stone, etc. I use a heart shaped stone to remember to speak and listen with the heart.)

- **A bell or chime** to signal gathering the group in a circle and/or for timing the sharing.
- **The Five Wishes** (A Health Care Directive) Offered at Hospice or order online.)
- **Angel 'Ohana Personal Profile** (Information about each member in case of emergency) This document is discussed later.
- *A Year to Live* by Stephen Levine (order soon from Amazon)
- **Other books** you would like to share relative to the themes.
- **Notebook** for ideas and remembering.

Special Ingredients

A sense of adventure	A sense of humor
Trust the process	Trust yourself
Tears and Laughter	A box of tissues
Playfulness	Your call to invent
Patience	Or find a way out of feeling stuck
Creativity	Co-creation
Putting your heart into it	Lots of hugs / Lots of listening
Compassion	For yourself and others

The Format For the Introductory Gathering

The format for all meetings is introduced in the introductory gathering so potential members can experience how the meetings flow.

A talking item is passed around the circle for each member to hold while sharing. There are no comments, advice, or interruptions from the group. The best gift to the speaker is being heard. All meetings are played by heart when anyone needs special attention or more time to share.

- **We begin with 10 minutes of silence**. In this way we can relax and be with ourselves and each other in silence.

- **Check in time.** For this first gathering, everyone says their name. The group repeats the name 3 times. There is a little thrill to hear your name this way.
- **Theme of the Day:** What attracted you to the Angel 'Ohana? What would you like to receive? What would you like to give?
- **Gratitude Circle.** We end with sharing our gratitude for what happened in the group, for the organizer and host or how we feel about anything at all. We stand in a circle holding hands.
- **Logistics and topic for the next meeting**. Where, when and who for the next meeting. State the topic for the meeting. Ask if there are questions.
- Ask for a Contact Person volunteer. The person asks for a contact list with names, phone and email. Ask members to contact the Contact Person if they will not be at the next meeting.
- Have snacks if you choose. Some groups meet in the morning and stay for potluck lunch.

PART FIVE

THEMES AND GUIDELINES FOR MEETINGS

All real living is meeting.
Martin Buber

The first two meetings are about getting to know each other and introduce ways to give and receive support.

A request to support you and the group:
- *Make your presence in the group one of your top priorities.*
- *The content of the meetings is not random. The sequence is arranged to deepen our bonds of trust and friendship. Each meeting is a steppingstone to the next. If one is missed you may experience a gap in continuity.*
- *If you are unable to attend a meeting notify the Contact Person.*
- *Vow as in Las Vegas "What happens in the circle stays in the circle."*

First Meeting: Getting to Know Each Other

The first meeting comes after the gathering to share the purpose of the Angel Ohana, answer questions and introduce members to each other.

We do not believe in ourselves until someone reveals that something deep inside us is valuable, worth listening to, worthy of our trust, sacred to our touch.

*Once we believe in ourselves we can risk curiosity, wonder,
spontaneous delight or any experience that
reveals the human spirit.*
e.e. cummings

Often people don't know each other when groups begin. It's always inspiring to see the bond of caring and trust slowly take the place of being strangers or casual acquaintances. This is a testament to the growing need in the world today for us to come together, pool our resources and collective experience. In this way we begin to dispel the illusion of separation and begin to *live* our inborn connection.

Listening is the gift of attention and opens us to connect. Casual conversations often miss the purpose of both people feeling heard. An open interest is possible when we don't interrupt, give advice, or try to think of what we're going to say. When we listen without inner or outer comment the air is clear of judgment. Simply listen and you will also be heard.

Facilitator: Welcome new members. Make sure new members have *Deepening Our Connection* as an overview of purpose and to use as a guide for the meetings.
Ten minutes for the Silent Time.
First Check In:
If there are new members ask them to share:
What attracted you to The Angel Ohana? What would you like to receive and what would you like to give?
Other members:
This is the time to share what's most important to you right now and how you feel today.
This lets the group know how you are in the moment.
In this way we begin to learn more about each other.
If you have nothing to share that's OK too. Just pass the talking item and we will come back to you when you are ready.

(Facilitator: State the format and the topic for the day. After a few meetings everyone will know the format. Always state the topic of the day.
Before Triads Of Listening read the e.e. cummings quote above.

Directions For Triads of Listening
Facilitator Comments:
"Come into triads. Discover something about each person in your triad you'd like to share when you come back to the circle. Two people listen to each person share. One question to ask: **What is most important to you at this time of your life?**
Listen with your heart, with your eyes and take in what is being communicated beyond the words. Listeners please don't comment, or converse. This way you can listen more deeply.
Each person has about three or four minutes to share in the triad depending on group size. A bell will ring when it's time to go on to the next person.

Come back into the circle and share what you learned about each person in your triad. There will be two people telling what they learned about each person. You don't need to share word for word. Just share your impression of what was said.
After all triads have shared ask if anyone would like to add to what was said about them.

Remember to save 10 or 15 minutes for The Gratitude Circle.
Logistics for the next meeting: Who, When, Where? I recommend meeting at the same time of the month and the same time of day.

Next Meeting
Ask if new members will be attending the next meeting. **This is usually the last time new members are added.** The group can discuss adding new members. (If there are more than ten members, I suggest asking a person to be a timer. Find in Guidelines for Facilitators)
If new members come after this meeting you may want to repeat *Getting to Know Each Other* at the meeting. Be sure to change people

in the triads. (Some groups like this process and want to repeat it the next meeting with a different triad.) If this doesn't apply go to the next topic: Asking For and Receiving Support.

Second Meeting: Asking for and Receiving Support
Most of us find it difficult to ask for or receive support. Men and women in general have a different set of rules. Women are "supposed" to take care of everyone else. This means they put their own feelings and needs aside. Men aren't "supposed" to need anything due to cultural expectations of being strong and independent. Women are used to being the caregivers and when it's our turn to receive we hide the fact we're in need. Some of us feel guilty; some feel shame when it's our turn to ask for support. Guilt happens when we think we've *done* something wrong; shame happens when we believe something is wrong with us. Either way we're left with unmet needs. Instead of feeling quilt or shame its time to give ourselves the kindness we give to others.

In the wisdom years our needs become increasingly real. Our families may no longer be alive or live far away. Our children and other relatives have their own lives and may need to care for their children.

Giving and receiving support is not a given. There are many ways to do both. We need each other to *learn how* to give and receive support in ways that deepen our trust. The "how' is a dance in each moment of giving and receiving. When we learn to ask for what is needed and receive what is offered we create a bond of gratitude between giver and receiver. Remember, "The gift to the giver is to be received."

First Round of Sharing: Read the meaning of 'Ohana in the preface.
What does belonging to an 'ohana mean to you? How is this different from your experience of other kinds of groups or families?

Second round questions are:
How do you feel about asking for support?

Do you have difficulty receiving support?
(Good time for facilitator to model the response by speaking first.)

Open Discussion
How can we assure each other its OK to ask for support? This is an open discussion. Ideas will come that are unique to the group.

Facilitator Comments:
Often someone will suggest meeting one or one with each member. If not, suggest the Buddy System. Below is how it's put into practice: "Let's begin with setting up a Buddy System. Chose a person to be your buddy who lives close to you that you don't already know. You can have tea, go for a walk or whatever you like. This is a good time to discuss support and what's most difficult for you about asking for support? Some members find it's difficult to ask for a ride to the airport. Others say they don't ask for support when they are sick due to feeling shame for poor health.
Members share their Buddy experience during the check in at the next meeting.
Choose a new Buddy after every meeting.

My Experience
My buddy and I had a walk and talked about what was on our minds and in our hearts at the time. We talked about our reluctance to ask for support. We made a vow to call when we needed to talk, or cry, and especially for needs we often keep to ourselves. We discovered we both hold on to our deepest needs. Then we agreed that was the time to reach out by saying, "I have a need and feelings about expressing that need." We also agreed we want our buddy to just listen with empathy and ask, "Is there any more you'd like to say?"
Remember, one of the greatest gifts we can give is to listen. Listening is not about problem solving. It is about the blessing of our attention. It demands nothing and meets the need to feel heard with empathy. This is a blessing for both listener and speaker.

Next meeting: We begin with themes and topics relative to the later years. Questions in each topic give us a way to inquire together and learn about this time of our lives. This is a shared experience that brings our thoughts and concerns into the healing light of awareness.

* THEMES FOR THE MEETINGS *

THE WISDOM YEARS, AN ADVENTURE OF A LIFETIME
or
How to Age Without Getting Old

There is an introduction to each theme to set the tone for the meetings.

Introduction

"In the middle of winter I discovered within myself an invincible spring."
Albert Camus

The Adventure of Added Years in the Second Half of Life

Not too long ago it was rare to live to the ripe old age of fifty. Today people are living longer and the years from fifty onward are another lifetime to explore. What will we do with these added 25 or 35 years and still counting? They could be a burden or a gift to open with curiosity and anticipation.

By trying to control the natural flow of aging and change we bury our bright minds in graves of denial. However, we can empower ourselves by taking our life into our own hands. With social connection we discover the common thread for healthy longevity.

With this gift of time when all is quickly passing by, we learn to let go of holding on and see what remains. Special lessons of this phase with the miracles of technology provide the attitude and the means for the later years to be a time of renewal.

Those of us in aging bodies know these years aren't for the 'faint-hearted'. It can be the most challenging as well as the most important time of our lives. We know by now we are not our bodies and can still embrace the body with kindness and gratitude. We are simply aware of what's happening with the body as the years pass by and learn to take care of ourselves and each other. This means even though the physical parts are aging we're getting stronger in spirit. So, let's dive in together, enjoy the wild ride and meet our later years 'without getting old'.

Aging in Other Cultures
Somewhere dancing around in my DNA imprinted with ancestral memory is a time when the later years were a blessing. Everyone looked forward to the time when life would change from the workday world for devotion to a spiritual life. Elders were honored and sought after for years of experience and the kindness of a heart tenderized by time. How other cultures engage with life tell us how they met their later years. Looking to this information offers another way to meet, perhaps enhance, this chapter of our lives today.

Australian Aboriginal Culture.
The Aboriginal people of Australia stand on over fifty thousand years of traditional ways. They can "remember" the Ice Age from stories passed down through generations. When I traveled through Australia, I was fortunate to spend time with some of these people still living the "old ways". I witnessed respect and affection for the Elders. The "Old Men" and "Old Women" are admired for years of skillful living. None that I met knew their age. They live in the eternal now of the Dreamtime.

Once I gained their trust I became a part of a family matrix giving me a place to belong. The matrix connects every one as an extended family that benefits the individual as well as the group. The elders pass down through generations the way to live, take care of each other and the land. I was blessed to have caught a bit of wisdom from these aging teachers before they too fade into Dreamtime.

Japan

Age in Japan is revered. A silk scroll tattered from years of use is so precious it is rolled up and saved for showing on very special days or tea ceremonies. A person of age or a work of art gathers meaning and beauty over the years. Living long and giving much is worthwhile and deserves admiration. Families take care of and appreciate all the elders have given of their lives over the years. The word, *arigato*, means more than "thank you". The closer meaning is, "Life is too difficult to live alone. Thank you for your presence."

India

A friend told me about his growing concern for his parents. In his perception they were slowly withdrawing from the life they had known. I told him about elders in India, there people look forward to being sixty when they can leave the responsibility of householder and turn to their inner life. Most become nuns or monks and devote the rest of their lives to spiritual practice. It seems to me the change my friend saw in his parents was right on time. Nature is wise when you leave it alone. The calming of outgoing energy and distractions of youth naturally slow down. Then we discover who we are beyond our previous roles. When people meet they say, "Namaste", "I greet the spirit within you." Spirit never gets old and seems to be dancing always.

Hawaii

I came into my grandmother years on the island of Maui where I met Uncle Harry. He was a humble and powerful Hawaiian Kapuna. One day I asked, "Uncle Harry, what does the word Kapuna mean?" "Kapuna means one who has lived life long and life has opened their heart." Now that's something to aspire to in one's life.

Uhane, is the innocence of the child that remains within each of us no matter how old the body becomes. I see this innocent and ageless spirit in my friends and have come to know that life is always new and in truth is never the same from moment to moment. Now we laugh more, play more, worry less and relax in the beauty of nature.

"Namaste Uhane", I honor the spirit and innocence within you.

The Wisdom Years

Giving Yourself What's Most Important to you is a valuable topic to explore. This topic can be revisited many times. What's important often changes as we change.

Meeting: Giving Yourself What Is Most Important To You *AT LAST*

> *The first thing upon which we should meditate is our*
> *precious and fleeting life, hard to obtain easy to destroy;*
> *I will now give it meaning.*
> Kalu Rinpoche

Facilitator Comments: (When you ask the following questions pass the talking item until someone is ready to share.) "Please look with your heart at these questions. Remember, "What is essential can't be seen with the eye."

First round of sharing: What are your beliefs about aging? How were these beliefs formed? In your experience are they true? How do you feel about this time of life?

Open Discussion:
What distractions still keep you from giving *yourself* the gift of your undivided attention? What busy habits and outdated roles fill the empty spaces?
What activities are you choosing *now* that have meaning for you?
What is *most* important to you at this time of your life?

Next meeting The Forever Changing You. No prep.

Meeting: The Forever Changing You

Aging is a fierce grace.
Ram Dass

As time moves on we come to know:
Beauty has little to do with our age. It has to do with aliveness and beauty within.
Self-worth has little to do with what others think of us. Self worth is taking care of ourselves, being kind to ourselves and loving ourselves and others without conditions.
Intelligence has little to do with brainpower. It is about listening to inner guidance.
Wisdom has little to do with being clever. It is being true to ourselves.
Health has a little to do with our genes. It has everything to do with a reverence for life and how we care for the life and body we've been given.
Peace of mind and body has little to do with acquiring material processions. Peace can come from letting go of the struggle with life and whatever no longer nourishes happiness.

First round of sharing:
What have you learned over the years that makes life more enjoyable and less stressful? (Please include how you learned and/or who or what experiences taught you.)

Open Discussion: What has changed in your life to give you more peace of mind? What nourishes your happiness at this time of life?

Next meeting: Surrender and Letting Go. No prep.

Meeting Surrender and Letting Go
Throughout our journey together we can share our experiences of holding on and the suffering it causes and what happens when we *let go.*
Change is one of our greatest teachers, always with us, always personal

and literally in our face. We can finally learn to befriend the changes and bend with the winds that come our way or get rigid with resistance.

In younger days my idea of surrender meant giving up. If what I wanted to happen didn't manifest letting go was failure. When my dreams and aspirations fell short of my expectations it was my doing and lack of know how. It never occurred to me that life has its own timing. The harder I pushed life to be the way I thought it **should** be the more I was stuck to what I was resisting. As I grew with the years I could see the crippling affect of throwing myself against the powerful flows of life. So, I surrendered and let go of trying to control life just being life.

Do I still hold on? Do I forget and try to control? You bet, until I remember I can choose not to suffer. When I'm not arguing with the situation, I'm more present to see solutions.
Surrender and letting go is really self-compassion. Willingly or unwillingly we have let go of our youth, our early ambitions and illusions. When the time comes we are asked to surrender to the loss of loved ones, to change itself and finally to let go of our bodies. This is a life-long practice. Sharing our process with friends can make these difficult tasks a tender experience.
.

First Round of Sharing
The best way to know if you are holding on is to become aware of tension in the body, How does holding on to what has already passed by affect you and your body? This includes people, events and thoughts...especially thoughts about those things you can do nothing about. This is called worrying. What do you still worry about? What have you finally *let go*? Share with the group how you did this and how you feel now.

Using the Breath to Let Go
Regardless of the cause, stress and pain reside in the body. We can begin to let go of this tension when we give our body attention and use our breath to let go.
Facilitator Commnent: (Go slowly as you give directions.)

"Close your eyes and take a few minutes of silence to discover where you're holding on. Are you holding on to your breath?.....Scan each part of the body. If there is tension or holding in the body, take your attention there. You may want to place your hand where you find tension. (This part usually takes about 3 to 5 minutes).

Take a deep breath in through your nose and out through the mouth with a big sigh. Breathe into a place in the body where there is tension....breathe out with a long sigh through the mouth. Breathe in and let go on the out breath until there is a softening (give time here). Continue to breathe into any holding in the body and let go with each out breath."
(Give the process about five minutes or until there is a peaceful feeling in the group.)
"Take time to open your eyes and continue deeply breathing."
Ask if anyone would like to share their experience.

Preparation for the next meeting: Gems of Vitality and Healthy Longevity
In preparation for the next meeting, write down questions about maintaining your health and wellbeing.

Preparing for Sharing Our Gems:
Remember we are the best teachers and guides for this subject. Who could know better what we need to know and what else we want to learn? You can use the following questions to prepare for what keeps you healthy and vibrant. Please bring information about resources and services provided for the older population in your community. Also bring names and contacts for health practitioners you know and what they have done for you. Also bring books or names of books and programs that have been helpful and have enhanced your attitude about aging.

Questions to assist in sharing your Gems:
- What is your personal "fountain of youth"?
- What ways have you learned to *listen to the needs of the body*?

- What techniques have you found that keep your body flexible and lively?
- What gives you a flexible and lively mind?
- What new information have you learned about health from the challenges of aging?
- Have you taken the care of your health and well being into your own hands? How have you accomplished this? What are the results?
- How has nutrition and exercise affected your health? What did you learn?
- How has humor played a part in your health? Please show us and we will laugh with you.
- How has gratitude and attitude played a part in your wellbeing? Tell us how, either positive or not.

Please share what you have learned or come prepared to give your "*gem*" as a group activity. This could be food and recipes, exercises, yoga, self-healing techniques, skin and hair health techniques, essential oils and tinctures, dance (bring you own music), singing (lead us in song), laughing meditation, and anything that is working for you. If you can, please keep your sharing to five minutes. There are exceptions for group activities.

The Gems of Vitality and Healthy Longevity

"*We cannot separate the health of the individual from the health of the family, the community and the world.*"
Patch Adams

"*Beware of false knowledge, it is more dangerous than ignorance.*"
G.B. Shaw

Good health is the number one wish especially as we age. The health of body, mind and attitude are profoundly linked. Psychologists and social scientists tell us healthy longevity has more to do with meaningful connections than the newest anti-aging technologies. You have already taken the first step toward good health by being in this group.

Taking Responsibility

An integral part of maturing or just "smelling the coffee" is taking responsibility for our health and wellbeing. No problem now, for our bodies come up with something new everyday demanding some kind of response if not our full attention. How we respond to these challenges can make the difference between diminishing our lives or opening up to a whole new world of opportunity for the best health and well being.

New Adventures in Health

This very body that is changing can become one of our greatest teachers for how to age without getting old. Good health is essential to renewed energy and meeting the day with a sparkle in your eyes.

The following topic gives us a foundation for sharing our Health Gems. There is time in every meeting to share what you're learning, what you've tried, what worked and didn't work and the results. Members often share new information by email as new info comes across the web. So here we are… resources and a research team of our own for healthy longevity and a happier way of living as our bodies change with time.

Meeting Sharing our Gems of Vitality and Healthy Longevity
Facilitator Comment: Share your gems for health with the circle. Group experiences may take more time. If the sharing is longer continue at the next meeting. (Pay attention to the time since there are two rounds of sharing. Let the circle know how much time is left for sharing after check in.)

My Health Gems

I'd like to share my Gems of Health and vitality with you as I would in a group. It took a lifetime to realize the importance of what did and didn't belong in my body. Using what I learned was a matter of mind over habit. I began by increasing the amount of water I drank everyday by taking sips even if I wasn't thirsty. Holding the water in your mouth for a few seconds lets it absorb throughout the body. Most of us are dehydrated causing ill health and just not feeling flexible and juicy.

There are three main gems that have given me greater health. These precious gems are close friends, an open and curious mind, and learning how to be healthy in a forever changing body.

I'd like to share the following gem because so little has been done regarding food to prepare us for healthy aging. There is already information about menopause, exercise, and attitude. Here is a gem I found that really worked for me:

The secret to better health and greater vitality as we age is **fewer calories and more nutrients**. Nutrient rich food is the key to more energy and less body fat. Without enough nutrients our cells don't get fed and the calories turn into fat. Since we aren't as active as we were in youth we need less calories and more healthy food. If we don't get nutrients daily our bodies actually starve. We eat more trying to satisfy our hunger for food our bodies can use. This is an essential key to "aging without getting old".

What are these foods, how do we maintain the nutrients and at the same time take care of a more sensitive digestive system? Food low in calories and rich in nutrients are fresh vegetables, fruit, and some whole grains. Fish, lamb, eggs, poultry, nuts and seeds are good sources of protein. Beans, brown or black rice, Tofu (not for everyone) have protein.

The preparation is key to maintain the nutrients. How to choose, store, prepare, and dress these foods for tasty, healthy eating can be found in the following:

The World's Healthiest Foods (winner of the National Best Books Award) and the website, whfoods.com by George Mateljan and a variety of other books and websites.

I have been eating this way for ten years and enjoy every meal with a bonus of losing fifteen pounds over time. To my surprise, I'm healthier and have more energy than in earlier years. More energy makes more exercise possible. Just walking everyday for 20 to 30 minutes elevates metabolism generating more energy to build muscles and burn fat.

These are my gems for nourishing my life force.

Next Meeting: The Five Wishes, A Health Care Directive. Please read over the directive and DO NOT fill it out. We will go through it as a group, share our responses, questions and information. This document can be purchased by calling 1-888-594-7437 or online at: www.agingwithdignity.org. Most Hospices have copies for $5 a piece.

Meeting The Five Wishes a Health Care Directive
The Five Wishes is a living will to be used when you can't make choices for yourself due to being on life support because of coma, brain injury or serious illness. This document protects family and friends from having to make difficult decisions without knowing your wishes. If you are concerned about being kept on life support a long time you can make choices now and state the circumstances. The Five Wishes is a legal document in most states in America. If it isn't legal where you live ask your local hospital or hospice for a legal health directive. You may want The Five Wishes notarized even if legal where you live.

Discussing the directive in the group gives time and thought to every section. Group interaction brings up questions, feelings and insights and often takes several meetings to complete.

I suggest choosing at least one person in the group to be your Health Care Agent. She will understand the directive and the reason for your wishes. Be sure each agent understands the directive and agrees to stand by your wishes. Give a copy to each agent as well as your doctor or health care professional.

It is imperative to discuss your directive with *all* family members. Any family member can override the directive by threatening the doctor with a lawsuit. Most doctors will back down. If there is such a probability, it is important to discuss the situation with your doctor and health care agents.

How to approach older children and family members often comes up. I talked with two of my adult children about The Five Wishes with an explanation of its importance to me. I also asked if they would like a Health Care Directive for themselves and their family. If so, I offered the Five Wishes. I also said I could be with them when they fill it out due to my experience with The Angel Ohana. This is a good time to ask if they would like to go over your directive so they will know your needs and wishes.

Next meeting: The Family of Angels Personal Profile. Make a copy of the Personal Profile and fill in. (The Profile is on a separate page for copying.) Bring 2 copies to the group. Keep 1 copy for yourself. For Check-in, include being with your buddy and what you did together. It is always builds friendship to say a few words of appreciation about your buddy.

Meeting The Angel 'Ohana Personal Profile
The Personal Profile is used in case of emergencies, if someone is ill or recuperating from an operation and needs support. Please fill out and give a copy to at least two people in the group. If you have become buddies with someone who lives close to you that would be a good choice. Another person in the group would be the person you chose to be a health care agent when we completed the Five Wishes. Some groups give all the profiles to one person to keep them on file. That person would be called for a member's profile when needed.

First Round of Sharing:
Share any special needs about being called upon for support. Such as, "I can't drive at night. Please don't call after a certain time. I don't like talking for a long time on the phone. I'm allergic to cats. I can't walk up and down stairs." Etc.

Open Discussion
Please discuss and ask questions. Some members want to be sure everyone knows where they live. Please discuss the logistics of this request and how to implement. Add anything else you would like on the Profile or what you would like to delete. This may give others ideas they would like to include or delete. Also discuss who will keep the profile.

THE ANGEL OHANA PERSONAL PROFILE

NAME
BIRTH DATE

ADDRESS
PHONES, HOME AND CELL
EMAIL

ANGELS LIVING NEAR YOU
YOUR HEALTH CARE AGENT NEAREST YOU
    PHONES AND ADDRESS

CONTACTS OTHER THAN ANGELS

IN CASE OF EMERGENCY CALL:
NAMES, PHONES and RELATIONSHIP
WHO HAS KEYS TO YOUR HOUSE OR WHO KNOWS WHERE HIDDEN?
WHO HAS YOUR FIVES WISHES?
    PHONES AND EMAILS

PETS: NAME AND KIND
WHO TO CALL AND VETERINARIAN
    PHONE NUMBERS

DOCTORS: NAMES AND PHONE
INSURANCE: NAME AND PHONE NUMBERS
ADDITONAL COMMENTS ABOUT:
    YOUR STATE OF HEALTH
    SPECIAL NEEDS

PLEASE FILL IN THE ABOVE. DELETE WHAT YOU'D LIKE TO LEAVE OUT. ADD WHAT YOU LIKE. GIVE A COPY TO A LEAST 2 MEMBERS OF YOUR ANGEL GROUP. MAKE SURE THEY KNOW WHERE YOU LIVE.

For members of the Angel 'Ohana only

Next Meeting: Hospice and Compassion and Choices. Facilitator will ask a member of Hospice to come to the meeting to talk about Hospice care. Become familiar with Compassion and Choices before the meeting. www.compassionandchoices.org
Come with questions to ask the Hospice representative.

Meeting Hospice Care and Discussion of Compassion and Choices
After the questions are answered, if there is time ask the group if they would like to discuss Compassion and Choices. Often members of Hospice are familiar with Compassion and Choices and can participate in the discussion. If they prefer they can leave at this time.

Facilitator Comments: Ask members if they want to become more familiar with the services of Compassion and Choices. This is a good time to discuss how members feel about what is being offered. If there isn't time continue at the next meeting.

Next meeting: Read the introduction to, *What is Your Cosmology?* This is something to contemplate before the meeting.

Meeting What Is Your Cosmology?

"The world is within you and the whole world is springing up from it."
Rumi

Introduction

Let's take a look at cosmology. This will initiate looking into your own point of view, thoughts and feelings of what life is about within the great mystery of the cosmic play. One definition of Cosmology is a study of the Universe in its totality and humanity's place in its magnitude.

Humans throughout the ages have created many stories and beliefs to go beyond the minds capacity to comprehend. We continue to try to fathom the mystery because it can affect our lives and everything we hold dear. This great unknown has been called by many names. God, the Universe, Spirit, The One, The Great Mystery are a few names humans have used since the dawn of consciousness. Carl Jung called this larger phenomenon the collective unconscious.

Just what is "this" all about? Is there a cosmic plan and what could it be? How do we play a part in the vast cosmic scheme of things? As you can see cosmology gives birth to many questions as we look with awe at the wonder of it all.

Open Sharing:
Respond to any question below or share what comes up from reading them all. The questions are a way for you to remember and perhaps share for the first time your own cosmology. You may also remember unexplainable experiences and how they affected you.

1. What is your Cosmology, your universal point of view? Where did you come from and where are you going? What brought you to know this?

2. Do you play a part in the cosmic scheme of things? What is that part as you see it?

3. If you are a part of the "Cosmic Soup" are you at effect of it or do you have a choice of how you respond? Perhaps it is a dance between the two.

4. How do you feel when you look at the stars or the Milky Way and beyond?

Next meeting: Continuation of Cosmology, Near Death and Mystical experiences.

Meeting Continuation of Cosmology
Mystical Experiences. Near-death Experience.
It's amazing how many of us have such experiences that are never or rarely shared with anyone. When I began telling others about my out of the ordinary events they also had remarkable experiences to share with me. We don't have to understand what they mean or

even how they happen. All we need to know is that they did occur and were important enough to leave a lasting impression.

First round of sharing: Choose one or more to share in the circle:

1. Mystical experiences
2. What is a mystical experience? What made this experience a different event than usual?
3. Near-death experience
4. Connection with loved ones after they died.
5. If reincarnation is true for you please share how you came to this conclusion.

Group discussion
The sharing may invoke further questions. Such as: "I'd like to know more about what you said. It's given me another way of seeing and I'd like to know more about your experience."
(The group may choose a second meeting for this topic.)

My Near-death Experience
While in a coma due to illness at age six, I learned how to die. As contrary as it may seem I simultaneously learned how to live.

I awakened in the top right corner of my bedroom. Looking down at a small sleeping body I could see the skin was red and long dark hair was spread out on a pillow. There was a knowing this body was my body although very far away. As I became aware of what I was seeing there was no fear, no doubt, no wishing to return…there was no emotion or thought at all. There was no attachment… just seeing what was so without comment of any kind. I was more consciously aware outside the body than I have ever been when in the body. Silence and stillness surrounded the moment.

It took me most of my life to realize what had actually happened. I was free of the usual conditioning of the mind that can cause fear around dying.

Next meeting: Contemplating our own mortality. We will use *A Year to Live* by Stephen Levine as a guideline. Purchase the book (amazon.com for $11) before the next meeting. Bring a Journal for notes and questions.

EMBRACING OUR MORTALITY AND AWAKENING TO LIFE

Introduction

"When we finally know we are dying,
and all other sentient beings are dying with us,
we start to have a burning, almost heartbreaking sense
of the fragility and preciousness of each moment and each
being, and from this can grow a deep, clear,
limitless compassion for all beings. "
Sogyal Rinpoche

Stephen Levine says, *"If death is the enemy life is a struggle."* Perhaps it's time to embrace our own mortality.

I've been asked why I chose *embracing* in relationship to our mortality. Embrace means bringing something in close and include it as a part of your life. I remember reading about monks who meditated in graveyards and on skeletons. Now I understand why. Coming closer to death we become more intimate with life. I realized in order to live without fear and love deeply I must finally embrace my *own* mortality.

Death is the crucible of making a fully human being.
Stephen Jenkinson

This is one of the most introspective and deeply healing sections of The Guide. Not because someday we will die, because when we embrace our own mortality something in us comes to life. What could be happening? How is it when we acknowledge the reality of death we become more vividly alive? This is when the book *A Year to Live* came to me. I was finally ready. This part of The Guide may touch something in you that is ready too.

The Angel Ohana offers the safety to explore what our culture has taught us to fear. When we attend to what we fear with mercy, the heart is involved and doubts are calmed. This embrace takes us beyond the surface of our lives where we open to the mystery of life and death and allow the heart to weave them together as one.

Although we may feel uncertain about entering the unknown, we have a place where matters of the heart are given attention. Our usually untouched questions, doubts, and fears are welcome and received as deeply as they are shared.

This theme offers a path of inquiry. Your own experiences, feelings and questions regarding this sensitive subject are an integral part of our exploration. Books in this theme are used to inspire introspection. They do not propose any particular teachings or spiritual and religious practice.

A Year To Live by Stephen Levine was chosen as a reference for this section. It is a simple and gentle approach to the sensitive content that follows. Stephen's poetic words of wisdom tell us that tending to our mortality with kindness and awareness can resolve our denial of death as well as our denial of life.

The Grace in Dying, How We Are Transformed As We Die by Kathleen Dowling Singh

Lovingkindness by Sharon Salzberg is a beautiful addition to read. *Who Dies* and *Unattended Sorrow* by Stephen Levine are also recommended reading. *Tao Te Ching The Book of the Way* by Lao-tsu is a book that stays with you for life.

Letters to a Dying Friend, What Comes Next by Anton Grosz

When Things Fall Apart by Pema Chodron

The Flowering of Grace poems by Denise Diamond This book was written as the author was dying and the transformation she experienced.

Why Give Attention to This Part of Life?

The unavoidable fact that we all eventually die is well known. Dying and death is also less known about or prepared for than any other part of life.
Bodhi Be

Death isn't an outrage.
Ram Dass

There are cultures and spiritual traditions that encourage preparing for death throughout life. There is a depth of aliveness and compassion present in these people. Just look into their eyes and see.

In western society some people think dealing with life is more than enough. "Why give attention to an event at the end of life we can do nothing about." However, when death comes everyone is deeply affected. Hearts can break when those we cherish disappear from our lives. We are unprepared and feel afraid because death can cause the unfathomable pain of loss. Perhaps loss is also caused by denying our own mortality or by rejecting both the beauty and darkness of what it means to be alive. We can't direct the show. We can only participate in the extraordinary gift of having a life to live.

Then there are people who believe death is a part of the cycles of life. The cycles of seeds, the cycles of the moon, the cycles of seasons and humans leaving their bodies are seen as the same. Are we different from everything else in the universal pattern of life coming and going and coming again?"

Due to our industrial-techno society, we have moved on from cycles to linear thinking. With linear thinking there are beginnings and endings. With endings there is loss. Whatever our beliefs may be, when we hold on tightly to life and our loved ones, perhaps it's the joy of loving that dies.

Topics in this section do not attempt to cover the vast spectrum of this subject. Your experiences and suggestions for inquiry are welcome. If you find something that gets your attention in *A Year to Live* or other relavalent books and experiences please share them and discuss with the group.

The following topics and questions can encourage attending to what seems unapproachable. Together we enter the mystery.

Topics For The Meetings

"Look with your heart. What is essential is invisible to the eye."
Antoine de Saint-Exupery

Inquiry in this section is intended to awaken your own innate wisdom. Questions request a response from the heart in all its depth of knowing. This means don't "think" about it. Just look within and see. Take your time for this is unexplored territory in our society.

Meeting How Do You Relate to Your Own Mortality?
I purposely use the word *contemplate* for the following process. Contemplation here means to consider a subject calmly without making decisions and allowing the mind to relax. This kind of inquiry is used throughout this section. Do we *contemplate* our mortality? This is a different experience than 'thinking about' death and dying.

Facilitator: "Close your eyes, go inside to a place of silence." (take a moment) "In that quiet space within, contemplate your own mortality. (take a moment) Notice what happens...does it touch something in you that feels unsure or resistant? (Take a moment.) Does it affect you in a way you find surprising?" Give 5-6 minutes for the whole process. If you feel the group is going deep, give a few minutes more.
Pass the talking item until someone is ready to share.

Next meeting: Read the introduction and Chapter 1 in A Year To Live by Stephen Levine. For Contemplation: If you have a year to live, how would you live your life?
Meeting If You Have A Year to Live How Would You Live Your Life?
Facilitator Comment: "Please share your thoughts about the introduction and chapter 1. Please read the part that touched you or you'd like to discuss."

First round: If you have a year to live, how would you live your life? What would you let go? What would remain? What would you do that you're not doing now? What keeps you from doing what you'd like to do now?
These questions can take two rounds of sharing. Thoughts and feelings come up after the first time around. Keeping your response to these questions in your journal allows seeing how they progress through the years.

Next Meeting: read chapter 2

Meeting "We die the way we live."
When we take this idea to heart we may pay more attention to how we live. With compassion for ourselves as well as for those we love, we know there is work to be done to complete what's unfinished. Perhaps you would like to live in peace and die at peace with your self, your relations and with life as it is. Is this possible? It is a gentle gift to those close to you as well as to your self and to all those you'll never know. Let's look at how we live with this in mind.

First Round of Sharing:
"We die the way we live."
What does this quote mean to you?
Consider how you live now and ask yourself how you might die. This takes courage to be honest with your self without judgment or analysis.
(This question is asked again at another time so you can notice what's changed.)
Group Discussion after sharing is complete.

Next meeting: Preparing to Die Chapter 3

Meeting Preparing to Die
Chapter three gives us an understanding of how we can literally come to life by preparing for our death. Preparing for death isn't about later it's about *now* for no one knows the moment of death. Even if you have years to live, why wait to embrace life or death?

When you begin to prepare for the time of dying and death, life becomes a teacher for letting go. An abundance of ways to experience this surrender can prepare us for the ultimate letting go of our body. Many teachings tell us what's on the other side. It's a matter of choice as to what rings true for you or if it remains a mystery. What we do know is the moment we begin to prepare for death, life can become a living experience of forgiveness, gratitude and letting go of all the various ways we try to control.

This may sound like a dichotomy, however, some people find *embracing* their own mortality profoundly wise. Perhaps now is the time to prepare for death and see what it teaches us about living. Are you living with "Yes" to life on your lips? Can you love with the greatness of your generous heart? Is forgiveness of yourself and others still lingering in shadows waiting for your merciful attention? Perhaps you're still holding on to anger for the loss of dreams or for life's unfairness.

First round of sharing:
Look within to see what's needed to heal what remains unloved and unloving to prepare to leave this life complete as you can. If you can look without judgment you will see more clearly. Could it be a matter of letting go rather than doing more?
(Facilitator: Give a 1 or 2 minutes here) Pass the talking item or share first if you like.)

Second round:
If you look with honesty is there still denial of your own death? Does becoming aware of this denial change your relationship to death and to life? Close your eyes and look within to see. (Facilitator: Give a 1 or 2 minutes) Pass the talking item or share first if you like.)

The Next Meetings: The next four meetings are about fear.
There are different kinds of fear: fear of pain, fear of death and/ or dying and fear of fear itself. These topics may take more than one meeting.
We'll begin with chapter 7 Fear of Fear. Form personal questions while proceeding through the "Fears". Share what stands out for you in these chapters.

Meeting The Fear of Fear
Beliefs about fear are formed by early conditions even before we are aware this is happening. We try to avoid fear for it can cause pain in our body and distract our mind. The fear we'll come closer to usually lies unattended in the shadows. It is this shadow itself

we ignore hoping it will go away. Running away seems to feed this painful emotion and in the long run it comes back with a vengeance.

With mercy for my human vulnerability can I *be* with the fear without being caught up in the emotion. When I don't think *I am* the fear I can get some distant from it. Then I can care for myself as I would for a child that is feeling fearful.

I haven't found a better way of facing this emotion and all it's causes than giving attention to the small voice that says, "Don't hurt me." Investigating this feeling together gives us the support we need to look into the causes of fear and release it's tight hold on the body and our gentle hearts. Have you noticed fear does not exist in the present? It only exists in the past as a story or in the future as "What if?" At the moment of a potential "train wreck" we're too busy taking care of the situation to think about being afraid.

First round of sharing: group discussion
Respond to the questions that ring true for you:
    Are you afraid of feeling fear?
    Where do you feel fear in the body?
    Do you judge yourself for feeling fearful?
    Do you shut down to control the fear? What is your usual way to deal with fear?

Second round of discussion:
    Can you be with fear without getting caught up in fearful emotions? What happens when can you be with the fear without trying to push it away or get rid of it in some way?
    Are there times when you can become more aware of how you relate to this state mind? Is it possible to have compassion for yourself with this awareness?
    Please give examples so we can learn from your experience.

Facilitator: Ask a member to slowly read The Soft Belly meditation: Page 32 in A Year To Live.

Next meeting: Read chapter 4. Dying From The Common Cold (The Fear of Pain)

Meeting Fear of Pain
If you have a headache, stump your toe or any other physical or mental "owie" what happens when you change it from "my" pain to "the" pain. Thoughts can also be painful such as, "I'm a complete idiot." or "The world is against me." Can you imagine these are not your" thoughts? Look to see if thoughts just come and go on their own. If this applies, please share your experience in one of the rounds of sharing.
First round of sharing:
If it serves you please share if you are in physical or emotional pain now.
If you are in emotional pain where do you feel it in the body?
If you are not in pain share what was meaningful to you in this chapter.
What beliefs about pain where you taught as a child?
Does saying *the* pain instead of calling it *my* pain make a difference in your experience?

Facilitator Comment: If someone is in pain give the person time to speak about their experience. Ask the group to be there with them in silence after they speak. Our spacious presence allows the person in pain to feel our compassion. Ask if they have a request for support. If the have a request the group can find a way to respond. (Rememer no advice, analysis or judgment from the group. If the member asks for specific suggestions they can be shared after the meeting.)
Some groups like to do a healing circle at the end of the meeting with members in physical or emotional pain. See Healing Circle directions in Guide For Facilitators

Second round of sharing:
At times we turn away from pain? What is the result when you turn away? What happens when you give the pain your undivided attention?
Next Meeting: Read chapter 10 Fear of Dying

Meeting Fear of Dying
1. We absorb many beliefs about dying from our culture, our community and often from our family. When we're older and wiser we begin to realize we actually *have* beliefs and some need to be revisited to see if they still apply.

Form dyads and take turns answering the questions. Facilitator will ring a bell for each partner to have five minutes of sharing.
First Round of Sharing:
What are your beliefs about dying? What beliefs are no longer true for you? What beliefs still remain? Are they still true for you now?

2. Fear says we will not be able to let go of the body when the time comes. There is benefit in the practice of letting go now. Life gives us many opportunities. We are faced with loss throughout our lives. How we meet those losses teaches us to let go and have compassion for the grief for all that is passing away.

Change partners for this round. Each partner has five minutes to share.
Second round:.
Have you noticed ways you are practicing letting go in life? What happens when you hold on or believe you can't let go? Please share.

Next Meeting: Read Fear of Death chapter 11

Meeting Fear of Death

> *"As awareness embraces fear, control becomes less an issue,*
> *and the mind sinks into the heart"*
> Stephen Levine

Please share what is meaningful to you in this chapter. If questions arise please bring them to share with the group.

Open sharing. Choose questions below relative to you or make your own comments or questions about the fear of death.
Each of us has been exposed to death in many ways. Is there still a belief that it won't happen to you? Is this denial of death because of the fear? What is the cause of the fear?
Does the fear of death have to do with the fear of losing control? If so, what are you trying to control?

Open discussion
Is there a part of you that does not fear death?

Next Meeting: One More Day
Recently a book came to my attention called *For One More Day* by Mitch Album. I realized there are unspoken words and feelings I'd like to say to those who are no longer in my everyday life.
Recall someone you would like to have one more day to let them know what they did to enhance your life and how you feel about them now in preparation to do a process in the group.

Meeting One More Day
Would you like to spend one more day or even a moment with someone?
Perhaps friends, family and mentors of the past and present may not know how much they contributed to who you are today? Would you like to let them know you still remember them and how much you appreciate what they did?

First Round of Sharing
Share what you'd like someone to know how you feel about what they did for you. These are people that are no longer a part of your life now or are no longer alive.

Let the person know what they did.
How this person made a difference in your life.
Let them know how you feel about them now.

Second Round of Sharing
Perhaps this meeting will remind you to express your gratitude to people and loved ones.
We'll begin today with our Angel 'Ohana. This is a special Gratitude Circle and an opportunity to let members know what they have done or do that makes a difference in your life.

1. Each member writes his or her name on a small piece of paper. Put all the names in a bowl. Pick a name from the bowl. If you get your own pick another one. Each member gives gratitude to the person whose name they have drawn.
2. When you share your appreciation include:

What they did or do and how it affects you to this day.
How it made/makes a difference in your life.
Perhaps it fulfilled a need.
Let them know your feelings about them now.

Example: "When you responded to my sad feelings about the loss of my dog, I felt my heart melt. I felt all right crying about the loss of my dear friend. Thank you for understanding and for caring." (If I had just said, "You are so compassionate" the person would never know what she did and the affect it had or how I feel about her.)

Next Meeting: Read The Moment of Death chapter 12 and The Act of Dying chapter 13 and Dying Contemplation chapter 14. Be ready to share parts that speak to you.

Meeting Open Discussion of the Chapters and The Act of Dying Meditation

Chapter 12 and chapter 14 give us much to contemplate. Read sentences or a paragraph you'd like to reflect upon with the group. Share your own life experiences.

The Act of Dying is a beautiful meditation. The ultimate surrender is letting go of the body when the time comes. Stephen Levine has been with many people during their transition and is experienced with the process. We can choose to enter this meditation by fully accepting life as it is this very moment. Letting go of holding on to what has already passed can lead to a more peaceful life. This practice supports us in our lives and during our time of dying.

Read The Act of Dying two times: Different people could do each reading.

Next meeting: Preparing For Life Review / Read Renewing Evolution chapter 5 and Noticing chapter 8.

Meeting Preparing For Life Review

"The unexamined life is not worth living."
Socrates

Often we are so caught up in living our lives we forget to stop and notice how we are responding or reacting to what is happening. What life sends our way can't be controlled. Being aware of *how* we meet the situation can make the difference. Without our attention life slips by and we've haven't learned a thing about ourselves or how to meet life in all it's varieties.
Someone asked, "Who is your spiritual teacher?" I thought for a while then replied, "My greatest teacher in life is adversity." I surprised the one asking as well as myself with this answer and it's truth.
Misfortune, pain and grief can be wake up calls. At the tipping point of suffering I want to stop the world and have it be a way I won't feel pain, only pleasantness. When I finally step back from struggling with life I can breathe again. No longer entangled in

the event I begin to see life just the way it is. This awareness allows me to have mercy on myself for the heartaches.

Ask yourself, "What events in my life have formed who I am today?" Have you noticed, some of the most formative times have been when you felt grief, anger, or disappointment? Looking back, what did these painful events teach you? What wisdom came from times of adversity?

I'll share this event and lesson as if I'm in the circle with you. *Our dog, Pretzel was run over when my daughter was eleven. This painful event was her first heartbreak. I was suffering for her grief as well as for the loss of our pet. Then I realized I was so caught up in my own pain there was no one to be with my child and her overwhelming sadness. When I was able to be present with my daughter I could be fully with her in her sorrow. Sometime later I realized I could do the same for myself. I could actually be there for myself when loss, illness or pain came my way. Life became less fearful because I know eventually I can disentangle from the event and be the comforter I need. This experience accompanies me through out my life when I remember I can step back from suffering and have compassion for myself without suppressing the pain and sorrow.*

First Sharing
1. YOUR STORY What is an event in your life that caused pain, disappointment or sorrow? How did this adversity effect you and is still with you to this day?
    What were the lessons learned? What wisdom came from the suffering?
    Now that you know the story and how it is effecting the present - your presence- you have a choice of holding on to the story or letting it remain in the past. When you embrace what you learned, can you say with forgiveness and gratitude, "Adios old story and thank you for the lesson and insights?"
Second Sharing
1. AWARENESS There is an underlying awareness that simply observes events as they happen. This bright consciousness is often present in times of spontaneous insights or life

threatening trauma. The curtain parts for a moment and you see everything as it is in the clear light of pure awareness. What I mean by pure is there is no thought, no emotion or on going comment. Without these overlays awareness sees the way things are.

What moments of clarity do you remember at these or other times in your life?

Next Meeting: Life Review. Read chapters 17, 18, 19, and the Epilogue in *A Year to Live*.

Meeting Life Review

> *All your past except its beauty is gone,*
> *And nothing is left but a blessing.*
>
> A Course in Miracles

This section introduces gratitude and forgiveness as a practice that can become a way of life. When we practice both, we can let go of the past with gratitude for what was learned. It is the love and gentleness in our hearts we want to nourish for the wellbeing of ourselves and for all those we hold dear. Gratitude and forgiveness opens the way.

Gratitude Process

Facilitator: Read aloud and very slowly or make a recording of the Gratitude Process on page 82 in A Year to Live. End on page 83.

When I read the Gratitude Process I give time between each person or group named. Example: "Bring to mind a friend. Tell them how much you appreciate their care and kindness. Send them gratitude. When love has filled the space say goodbye as if you might never go this way again. (Take time here, then go to the next one.)

Bring to mind your parents, continue as above with each person named."

I always include, "Bring to mind your pet, all animals and wild life. Send them gratitude. When love has filled the space say goodbye as if you might never go this way again." (Take time here, then go to the next one.)

I also include, "Bring to mind all seen and unseen beings that have supported you all of your life. Tell them how much you appreciate their care and kindness. Send them gratitude. When love has filled the space say goodbye as if you might never go this way again." After the process, experiences can be shared in the circle.

If there is time, continue with the Forgiveness Process or wait until the next meeting.

Forgiveness Process
Facilitator: Read aloud or make a recording of the Forgiveness Process on page 83 in
A Year to Live. Begin with, "Bring to mind someone who caused you pain."
After the process, experiences can be shared in the circle.

Next Meeting: Self-forgiveness, Self-empathy, Self-compassion

Meeting Self-forgiveness, Self-empathy, Self-compassion
(The following processes can be done in one or two meetings.)

When Kitty Carlisle was asked her secret for long life she said, "Every morning I get up, look in the mirror and say, "I forgive you for EVERYTHING!"
Self-forgiveness
It has been said that forgiveness begins with forgiving ourselves. And what are we actually forgiving? Perhaps its that part of us that tries to protect the small "me" from feelings of rejection and hurt. We think if we can keep ourselves in line with self-critical thoughts then others won't be able to judge us. We might even get approval for being "good." Often we work hard to keep suffering at bay by using self-judgment when what we really need is self-empathy.

When we understand how we misuse judgment then it can no longer control our thinking. We can even have forgiveness for being so hard on ourselves. We are, at that moment, free of constant critical mind chatter. Although it may return we see it for what it

is; trying to control what we believe others will judge wrong. When we forgive ourselves forgiving others comes more easily.
Self-forgiveness Process
What we haven't been able to let go for years never seems as terrible to others and evokes compassion rather than blame.

Facilitator Comments:
Equal size slips of paper are given to each person.
Write down on the paper something you have done or said that you have never forgiven. Fold it and put it in a bowl. No one knows which paper is yours. Pass the container around and each person takes out one paper. If you get your own put it back and choose again.

- One at a time a person reads what is on the paper. After reading it say, "I forgive you." Most of the time (I've never seen it not happen) the person reading what is written can say, "I forgive you" and really mean it.
- Then in unison the whole group says, **"I forgive you!"**
- After the process: "Place your hands on your heart area. Take a few deep breaths. Look within to know how you feel now about the forgiveness you've been given in the Forgiveness Process. Has letting go of self-blame and guilt released you from a prison of self- condemnation?

Self-empathy and Self-compassion Process

You do not have to be good.
You do not have to walk on your knees.
For a hundred miles through the desert, repenting.
You only have to let the soft animal of your body
love what it loves.
Mary Oliver

Self-empathy can release knots in the solar plexus and move the armor away from your heart. Knowing it's natural to have feelings and needs is self-empathy. When you know what needs are trying to be met, empathy can take the place of "What's wrong with me or why am I so needy?" From a place of self-empathy it's possible to express a need with a request instead of a demand that carries an expectation of fulfillment.

Facilitator Comment: "Close your eyes and take a moment to remember something you said or did you haven't been able to forgive. Ask the following in order to give yourself empathy and forgiveness. (Go slowly with time between each sentence.)

- Ask yourself, "What need of my own was I trying to fulfill at the time of my actions?" Often there was a need to feel less fear or confusion. Beneath all the reasons is there a need for connection?
- Give yourself understanding and empathy as if you were a child or dear friend.
- Say to yourself, "If I knew then what I know now would I have done something
- Different?"
- Is there a request you can make of yourself for understanding and compassion for what was done?
- Thank yourself for bringing attention to this event in your life and appreciation for what was learned."
- You may like to share your experience with the circle.

Next meeting: Read chapters 23, 34 and 35
If you have comments or questions about these chapters share them at the meeting.

Meeting Surrender and Letting Go of Control

The Master sees things as they are,
without trying to control them.
She lets them go their own way,
and resides in the center of the circle.
Lao-tsu

A tattered leaf had fallen from a tree. Spaces left made a pattern of delicate silvery grey lace. In every phase of life we let go of something even if painful in the moment. What remains is beautiful.

Before you go another step in your life, now is a good time to begin letting go of holding on to what you believe is the way you and life should be. What can and cannot be changed will be revealed at the time. We notice everything changes on it's own anyway. We can flow along and pay attention or be bumped along, "Ouch!" from trying to have it our way. When we hold on tightly to what has already passed–which passes in every moment–we become rigid in body and mind trying to be in control of losing something that no longer exists (except in our own minds).

When I imagine my own dying, it is surrender to the inescapable experience of death that catches at my breath. Will I let go or will I hang on in the passing of life out of this body? For me this is suffering, to rail against the inevitable. How true this is in life. There is no suffering greater than being paralyzed in resistance to life passing by. Stuck in holding on, we completely miss the moment and any choice we might have to respond differently. There is compassion here for the human condition of both the struggle against life and the pain caused by holding on to the way we want life to be.

The first definition of surrender is "to give up, give in". Somewhere at the end of the list of definitions is "give way to". There is a part of our makeup called the ego, the little me, that is afraid of losing control. Let's go around the ego for a moment and ask, "What can we give way to and make way for something new?" Life gives us many ways to practice letting go making way for the new. Could dying be another surrender when we have practiced this all along? I'm not sure "letting go" or surrender gets easier just more familiar.

Group discussion: Use the questions to see what comes up for you.
What is the underlying cause of control for you?
Does fear have a part in wanting to be in control? What is the cause of this fear?
Do you feel helpless or relieved when you are not trying to control?

What are your experiences of surrender instead of arguing with life just being life.

Group Process
Facilitator Comments: "Close your eyes and feel into a place in your body that is tense with holding. You don't need to remember the cause of this holding? …….. Take a deep breath into the body and let go with the out breath…….. Take another deep breath and let go of holding on. Continue breathing and letting go." (Use your own experience to know when it's time to say).
"Gently open your eyes. Look around the circle. Notice how you feel."
"If you like, share your experience in the circle."

Next Meeting: Living In The Body read Chapter 21

Meeting Living In the Body and Letting Go

"Before we can leave the body effortlessly we have to inhabit the body fully." Stephen Levine

"Resistance is pain." Ida Rolf

We humans and other embodied beings have a natural determination to stay alive. We are attached to the body as long as it serves a purpose and even when it causes distress. Often we reside somewhere just outside of the body trying to escape physical or emotional pain or grief. It is this resistance that turns the pain into numb lifelessness.

Try the following:
Hold your shoulders or any part of the body as tightly as you can.
When the body begins to harden and hurt keep holding on against the pain.
Don't let go in fear of more pain.

Now, breathe deeply and let go of holding on with each out breath.

Keep letting go as you exhale. Notice what happens.

One of the best ways of experiencing the energy of aliveness is to bring attention to the body. If there is emotional or physical aching in the body, bring awareness to this discomfort as well. This awareness makes it possible to let go of what is held in the body/mind. After connecting to the discomfort it helps to let go with conscious breathing and letting go on the out breath. Sensations of lightness and expansion often remain in the presence of acceptance and compassion. Could this also be the way it is in our dying?

Body Meditation
You can record or ask a member to read "A Meditation On Life In The Body", page 104 in *A Year to Live*. Go slowly since it takes time to fully enter the body and feel the sensations.
Share how do you feel after this meditation? Has connection with your body changed? Does the ability to let go give you peace of mind?"

Next Meeting: The Ethical Will
Usually a will is one that states what items and property we want to leave people after we pass on. An Ethical Will is about values instead of valuables. It leaves wisdom, loving thoughts, and stories about what we learned from living.

An Ethical Will is an heirloom that can be handed down to future generations. A touch of love for those you'll never meet. This may be the most cherished remembrance you can leave to all who are left behind.
Prepare your Ethical Will. Please read parts of your Ethical Will at the next meeting.

Meeting Reading the Ethical Wills
Share Ethical Wills in the Circle. Someone could write down the most outstanding "gifts" from each person. A copy could be made to give everyone in the circle.

Facilitator Comment: "Did this process remind you of more "gifts" you can leave to others?"

I have included some gifts my mother left with me. "Remember, no regrets, only gratitude." Another one, "If you're going to feel guilty, don't do it. If you must do it don't feel guilty."
A story for my children and grandchildren: When I was young I thought being patient was anything but a virtue. I was sure nothing would happen if I didn't do it myself AND it had to be done right now. Later years tempered my impatience and I experienced a gentle timing when all I need comes to me when I'm ready to receive. I discovered where I place my intention, like aiming an arrow then letting it go, is what the universe sends my way perhaps in different packaging and in universal timing.

Next Meeting Read chapters 26, 27 in *A Year to Live* and chapter 15 in *Who Dies* by Stephen Levine.

Meeting Who Dies?

Let what comes come,
Let what goes go,
Find out what remains.
Ramana Marharshi

Who dies? This is one of the most profound and yet innocent question you can ask. Perhaps it's not a question to be answered. Just keep it before you and let it take you into wholehearted contemplation. It's a question to ask yourself throughout your life.

First Sharing
We have all experienced many small deaths within ourselves as we have moved through our lives. What was it that "died" at those times? What is it that remains?

Second Sharing **Facilitator Comment:** "Choose a partner to look at the next question together. We will have five minutes of silence before sharing with your partner. I'll ring the bell at five minutes to begin the sharing and again in ten minutes to end the sharing." Ask the question below **before** the five minutes of silence. (Facilitator participates in a dyad or triad. Keep an eye on the group to see when dyads are finished or need more time.)
Question For dyads:
   When we ask, "Who or what dies?" the next question is, "What remains?"
(I suggest writing down what comes to you in your journal. You may have more additions to your response to this question as the years go by and layers of identities fall away.)

Next meeting: Harvesting the Fruits of Our Journey, A Commitment to Life.

Meeting Harvesting the Fruits of Our Journey, Making an Alter to Life and Death
We have come far down a road not usually taken in our society. We looked deeply to discover our feelings, perhaps transformed how we perceive death and dying. Doubt and fear have come out of the shadows weakening their power. Embracing our mortality has deepened our connection by creating bonds of compassion for each other and for our fragile humanity.

When we contemplate our mortality we wonder what happens after we die. There are various ways to imagine or know without a doubt what happens after death depending on your culture or your personal perspective. Chapters 27, 28, and 29 tell us what we truly are is awareness and can never die. There are many ways to interpret what is being said in these chapters that may relate to your own beliefs or may also be true for you. You may want to share what is true for you in the first round of sharing.

First Round of Sharing:
Has sharing your thoughts and feelings about death and dying changed how you perceive your own mortality? What has changed? What questions remain?
Do you feel more gratitude and a deep connection with the wonder of life?
You may want to hear each person's thoughts about what happens beyond death in a group discussion.

Second Round: "You die the way you live". If you project to the future consider how you live now and how you might die. What has changed for you since this quote was investigated at the beginning of Embracing Our Mortality?

Next Meeting: Allow time at the end of this meeting to prepare for the next. Create what you would like to happen at the next meeting,
A suggestion: Make an altar with pictures of loved ones who are living and those who have died. Remember to include your pets. Also for the altar, bring something from nature where we find the natural cycle of living and dying so beautifully and visually expressed. Create a skit, dance, poem or song about life and death.

The celebration could also include a special way of expressing gratitude. One way is to stand in the Gratitude Circle and express your gratitude without using words. You can dance or use movement to express how you feel about your experience and the group. Some may also want to speak words of gratitude, say a poem or sing a song.

Meeting A Celebration of Living and Dying.
I give the poem *I Am Not I* to each member in the gratitude circle at the end of the meeting. The poem is copied in calligraphy and printed on paper that resembles parchment. I offer this poem in gratitude for the courage and devotion to embrace your own mortality and the healing this brings to all beings.

I AM NOT I

I am not I.
I am this one standing beside me.
whom I do not see.
Whom at times I manage to visit
and other times I forget.
The one who forgives,
sweet when I hate.
The one who takes a walk
when I'm indoors.
The one who remains silent
when I talk.
The one who will remain standing
when I die.

Juan Jimenez

PART SIX

DEEPENING OUR SUPPORT

The whole of the holy life is good friends. Our relationships – and our
love –
are ultimately what give depth and meaning to our lives.
The Buddha

Right here in this theme is when we earn our angel wings. As
we grow older we know we will need each other for big and
small needs and other "surprises". Our wings grow and hearts glow
from giving a foot massage, bringing chicken soup, or visiting a
member in crisis. We can offer to be a Medical Advocate when one
of us goes for tests, a biopsy or other procedures and need physical
and emotional support. Caring about each other can heal in ways
more than we know.

How we support each other is a work in progress and always subject
to change. As the years go by we learn how to care for and give our
support in ever deepening ways. Through the years we discover
needs are personal and how each are met is a co-creation among
the members.

Meeting Deepening Our Support

Discovering Our Needs
Very often we ignore our own needs. Women look to needs of
others and how to take care of them ASAP. Men don't like to admit
they have needs because they may be seen as weak. Let's take

time to look into our own needs and give them the attention they deserve. The most important need is to let others *know the need* so the appropriate support can be given.

The best way to give support is to ask what is needed. If asking doesn't' get a response ask a few questions about the situation and you will intuitively know how to begin. Advice is not necessary and takes the attention away from the person in need. The person may just want to get clear about their need by putting it into words. They may just want to be heard or need a hug or gentle touch.

Giving advice
Giving advice can cloud your intuition and a clear response to the situation. The person often only needs your presence. She may need to be heard and hear a response that let's her know you care and are simply there for what she needs.
Example: I visited a friend in hospital who had a knee replacement. There was so much pain in her knee that in her mind she had rejected the whole leg. She was unable to do the necessary physical therapy. Her need at that moment was to regain the use of her leg. I *asked permission* to touch her leg. I softly stroked and gently spoke to her leg and knee with the intention of reconnecting her to the leg. Within a half hour she was able to walk with assistance.

First Round of Sharing
What is a need you have right now regarding your health and wellbeing?
How can the group support you in getting this need met? Please make a **request** that let's members know what is needed.

Facilitator Comment: Remind members to hold their advice or comments about what they or others have done. Ask what the member needs and a request that could fulfill the need. Remember, a request is not an expectation. It can give clarity to what's needed.

Choosing an Angel Buddy and a Medical Advocate

The purpose of an Angel Buddy is for each member to have only one person to call when support is needed. The Angel Buddy finds a member who is willing to respond to the need. She is not expected to give assistance. Being able to call one person makes it easier for the member in need. This also helps her ask for support since there is *no* **expectation** for the Angel Buddy to fulfill needs. The Angel Buddy is mutually chosen between two members. The duration of the partnership is decided between the two members. Each Angel Buddy keeps a copy of their buddy's Angel Ohana Personal Profile in order to have the information.

It helps to have a phone tree so members only call one person. If the person called isn't able to help at that time she calls the next member on the phone tree. The member who can assist calls the Angel Buddy to let her know the need has been fulfilled. Often two or more people work together. If the Angel Buddy wants to provide what's needed, that's OK too.

A Medical Advocate is someone who accompanies a member to an appointment with a doctor especially for diagnosis, biopsy or other procedures. Since the Advocate isn't personally involved she can offer rational options for decision-making. She can organize group support before and after an operation. The Angel Buddy or another member could be an Advocate.

Open Sharing
Discuss the purpose of an Angel Buddy and an Advocate. Discuss how members in the group can fulfill needs as a team.

Next Meeting: Team Care Preparation
Read *Share The Care: How to Organize a Group to Care for Someone Who is Seriously Ill,* by Cappy Capossila, Sheila Warnock and Sukie Miller. (available at amazon.com)
The book tells how "sharing the care" supports the caregivers and ultimately the person in need. This is the groundwork for building team care.

The group may decide to read the book and look over the content in order to become familiar with the purpose of sharing the care giving. When the time comes to take action the group can come back to this section and make plans to proceed in order to share the care of a member in need. The group can also assist with a loved one of an Angel Ohana member.

Meeting Team Care
This meeting is about how to organize care for those who are terminally ill, chronically ill, disabled, recuperating from an operation or in the process of dying. It is comforting to know we can care for each other and be assured others will care for us without exhaustion or compassion burn out. We are blessed to have a family of friends who can share the work of care giving. This is when we earn our Angel Wings by sharing our heartfelt support and help maintain the dignity of our friends.

This is a good time to use CaringBridge. CaringBridge is an online interactive way for people who are seriously ill, terminally ill or disabled to stay in touch with a larger circle of friends and family.

www.caringbridge.org is a personal and protected site for friends and family to stay in touch with a person's health journey. Each person can write in a virtual guestbook that is read and can be responded to by the person who is ill. On this website photos can be posted. CaringBridge is a way to create a personal social network for those who are ill at no cost. When a person is close to dying someone else can write her story or write notifications. In this way people close and far away can stay in touch with those who are ill or terminally ill and be included in a caring circle of friends and family.

Caring Bridge also offers a Support Planner calendar to coordinate care and needed tasks as a group. Go to caringbridge.org and click on *SupportPlanner* to coordinate care and organize task by calendar. Click on *start* and follow the prompts. One person manages the calendar. This person calls members or they call her to add their name and task to the calendar. If you need help with this call 651-452-7940 or click on **contact**. Its easy once you get the hang of it.

Next Meeting: *Being With Dying* by Joan Halifax. The subtitle says it all: *Cultivating Compassion and Fearlessness in the Presence of Death.* I suggest one or several people volunteer to read the book *Being with Dying.* **(This suggestion can be used for any book or article relevant to any Theme. In this way group members can take turns reading books with special appeal for them and inform the group).** For those who read the book please share what touched you most. What did you learn about being with dying? Read sentences or paragraphs and discuss.

Meeting Being With Dying

I was visiting a ninety nine year old friend in a convalescent home. He realized he was finally in his last days and didn't want to prolong his departure with drugs and tubes. His friends and family wanted to keep him alive and ignored his wishes with the idea he was a bit demented. Clearly neither he or his family had prepared for his dying. Fear filled the room where compassion could have softened every heart. In his wisdom he wanted to let go of his ailing body in the peace of his own home with loved ones willing to say goodbye. I held his hands. The last words I heard him say were, "I'm so sorry, so sorry I'm so sick." I hugged his hands, "You're not sick. It's the body that doesn't feel good." A tiny smile came and then, "I love you all...goodnight...I'll see you later."

Speaking of death and dying with loved ones **before** the consuming work of dying is helpful preparation. Dying is a personal and intimate experience between you and nature. Like the butterfly, you can't hold back nor hurry the emergence from the cocoon. This way of being with dying requires heartfelt presence of all involved as the person makes peace with the process of letting go. Those who can follow the needs of the dying without personal or religious comments or advice can offer this special support. Some communities offer workshops in becoming a midwife for the dying.

First Round of Sharing: Members who read *Being with Dying* can share what you learned with the group. Read the parts that stand out for you. Ask for questions and discus.

Open sharing: Please share your experience with being with someone in their time of dying. Include what you learned and what could ease the passing for others and yourself.
After three minutes of silence, share how you would like your time of dying to be.

My Wishes For End of Life Care
As I am writing My Wishes for End of Life Care a beloved member of our community is dying. We rarely contemplate how this time of transition will be for ourselves. In our time of dying we experience one of the most important passages of our lives. I will share what I can with you for crossing this threshold is calling us to come closer. The following experience taught my heart what I needed to know to finally let go into dying.

I've just returned from a "farewell" circle for our friend who died last night. I thought I would just go, view the body, hug my friends and leave. A single stalk of Jasmine with a feather butterfly seemed perfect to put in the casket to honor her love of elegance and beauty. After I saw her peaceful body was covered with petals, I walked to my car down a long driveway, then turned around and came back to the house. I couldn't leave. A palpable field of energy was calling me to come in close. I could feel my heart opening and returned to hug everyone even people I didn't know.

As we gathered around my friend's body I spoke my gratitude to the team of caregivers and to those who made it possible to share her dying process across the Internet. The miraculous "inner net" gave people who knew her a way to become a part of the closer attending friends. Each caregiver who was with her in body as she was leaving hers shared their hearts during her times of struggle as well as times of letting go. We knew when she wanted a tea party or wanted to be carried outside to her garden. When asked what was keeping her alive, with passion she replied, "Beauty and my beloved grandson."

The caregivers shared by email the impact on each of them of how it was as she was dying, bringing the larger circle of friends in close even from a distance. Their words spread in waves across the community, then around the world, connecting us all when one of us leaves the body and enters our hearts.

Thank you my friend, for your generous teachings as you were dying in the arms of love. How beautiful it is to die this way.

When the Dalai Lama was asked what he would like to do next, he replied he was fifty eight years old and felt it was time to complete his preparation for death. Often our time of dying is relegated to the background of our lives even more than death. This is unfortunate for we can be taken by surprise with no preparation for this deeply moving and intimate experience.

Preparing for death begins with asking, "What am I willing to do in life that can bring tranquility and the ease of letting go to the experience of dying? Can the embrace of my own mortality teach me to live with forgiveness and gratitude and prepare me to meet the unknowable challenges when the time comes?"

.

These wishes are the beginning of preparing for dying. They are important for our caregivers and those we love. Often those last hours become a deepening with yourself, with those assisting you and ultimately with the fragility of life and all we love.

My Wishes For End of Life Care was written in response to having been with dying friends. Often family and friends and the person dying are unprepared for this inevitable part of life. Our culture has drifted away from this all consuming passage, forgetting how death and dying can awaken spirit and deepen the experience of love.

This time-like no other-is asking us to surrender what keeps us believing death is an enemy and love is too tender to feel. The immensity of life that death can reveal is beyond what the mind can conceive. Being at this threshold with another is a blessing, a gift for the heart to receive.

Meeting Wishes For My Time of Dying
Wishes for the time of dying are personal and come from our innermost nature. The way I see it leaving this body is the next most important event in my life. Being with dying friends opened my heart to see this is true for me and may be true for others. This is a subject for contemplation and discussion. If you are using the guide as an individual, one on one or with a family, this also applies. In this way we learn from each other before we complete our wishes.

Your wishes now may not be needed or possible to follow at the time. However, giving attention to this time in every life is a kind thing to do for yourself and those who love you. Letting go of the body is often all consuming work and can engage every part of you. Now, while the mind is calm you can contemplate how you would like this time to be. This is full engagement and calls for sensitive and compassionate support. The heart is free to meet the needs in the most loving way when we let it be known what supports us.

Open sharing
What are your wishes for how you would like to be cared for during your time of dying?
Are there special needs for comfort? What surroundings would you like?
Where would you like to die?
Who would you like to be your team of caregivers?

How would you like the body to be cared for after death?
If you have pets have you made sure they are cared for?
How would you like visiting friends and family to be cared for in their grief?
Please share other wishes of your own.

These are a few requests I'd like to share as if I was in a circle with you. I chose the same 3 health care agents in my Five Wishes to be with me during the intimacy of letting go of my body. I also chose 3 more close friends that at times know me better than I know myself. I know these Angel friends will stand by my wishes and create a field of love just by their presence.

I deeply care that my community can be part of my dying time and be included in the circle of friends and family. Not everyone can be at bedside. Caregivers and Hospice nurse and volunteers need to keep their focus. However email and Caring Bridge are ways to keep everyone informed day by day. Each caregiver can share their experience with others by email to let them know how I am doing and what I would share if I could. Contact is helpful to the caregiver team to let the next shift know what is occurring before they arrive. Friends and family near and far can be kept informed by email or Caring Bridge. See the meeting, Sharing the Care and www.caringbridge.org.

Be sure your Angels and heath care agents have a copy of your wishes attached to The Five Wishes. It's important to talk it over with them so they will understand your wishes for your time of dying.

Additional Notes
Hospice Care
I'd like to add Hospice nurses provided skilled and compassionate care for our friend's last two weeks of dying.

Hospice provides palliative care and support for persons with a prognosis of having six months or less to live. The goal of hospice is to help patients live without anxieties, provide comfort and relief from pain and symptoms. A team of professionals, Hospice nurses and trained volunteers strive to meet the physical, emotional, social, and spiritual needs of each patient and family. Hospice is Medicare/Medicaid certified providing services at a patient's home, a nursing home, a hospital or other residential setting.

People I have attended in their last days of dying have called in Hospice. The Hospice nurses and volunteers support the patient and the family and the caregivers. Caregivers were advised how to care for the person when a nurse or volunteer is not in attendance. www.hospicecare.com for more information and to find a hospice in your area.

Compassion & Choices is a nonprofit providing free end-of-life consultation to patients and their families. Many choices for peaceful dying exist. If patients meet the guidelines and choose aid in dying, Compassion & Choices accepts that decision and offers continued consultation at the time of dying. They neither provide nor administer the means for aid in dying.
Call toll free at: 800-247-7421 or visit www.compassionandchoices.org
This interactive website provides information and documents you may find useful.
You can choose to be on the mailing list and be kept up to date.

Making Arrangements For The Body After Death
What to do with the body after you die takes contemplation. Making a clear decision *now* is a responsibility that relieves those left behind from making the choice. This isn't a usual or easy task while you're still alive. You may want to discuss this with your minister, priest, rabbi or spiritual teacher. Becoming familiar with the choices and services available in your community is helpful.

In my community of Maui, there is an unusual and caring "Undertaker" named Bodhi Be. This sensitive man with a rare humor offers goods and services to the dying and their families. His services include many choices of burial, coffins, urns, and other relative information. He also offers caregiver support, home funeral supplies, Celebration of Life ceremonies and many other services for personal choice.

You may want to revisit Disposing of the Corpse in *A Year to Live.* Chapter 33 reminds us that letting go of the body is an act of faith. Relinquishing level after level of holding on to the body frees the spirit to live lightly within it.

PART SEVEN

DEEPENING OUR CONNECTION

Why does your smile light up my eyes so?
Why does my heart continue to glow?
O, let the years pass slowly...slow
for there is much more of you
I wish to know.
Judith Small

Introduction

We have taken the first vulnerable and tentative steps toward companionship, support and contemplation of our own mortality. We have come to know connection is at the heart of it all.

Ask yourself, "How can I go beyond the surface of what's apparent and acknowledge my innate need for connection?" This question lingers in our hearts even though hidden away. How do we find ways to live in two worlds, a world of everyday survival and the other of deep resonance with everything that is life? Taking this question to heart, nurturing contact becomes real instead of lingering in the land of good ideas.

How to truly connect is often overlooked in our society. Our culture doesn't cultivate ways for the heart to be involved in everyday life. Perhaps we often miss the mark because we haven't created artful ways and practices to guide us there. Honoring this innate longing and the intention to "deepening our connection" brings us closer to this unspoken need.

At times I meet someone who lets down a protective wall to say, "I have been with many people in many ways and never found true connection. I have longed to have this experience in my work, with my friends, even with my mate. We just never quite meet in that place where there is a deeply felt resonance. I've found intimacy in sex, in truth telling or in compatible qualities and still that innocent timeless presence goes unmet. I long for that moment of simultaneous recognition."

Deepening Our Connection is the last theme of the guide. It's purpose is to develop deeper connections with ourselves, with each other and ultimately embrace a presence within greater than we believe ourselves to be. An intention of this magnitude could open to multitudes of opportunities to explore and discover. The journey before you can inspire spontaneous self-expression and perhaps moments of simultaneous recognition of that innocent timeless presence within us all.

The Meetings

One of the most important parts of this section is the interplay of co-creating the content of the meetings. The very act of collaboration goes beyond the "me" becoming "we." Using our collective wisdom guides the way. Giving birth of any kind calls out our strengths and resistances. So let's be patient and gentle with each other and with ourselves to protect the tender shoots of the creative process.

The content and format of the meetings is in the hands of the members. By this time you trust each other enough to be willing to try new ideas and see where they lead. You may want to have a "heart storming" meeting or several to decide where you want to go from here. After each topic is complete the group may need a meeting devoted to where to go next. Since this is a well functioning family, everyone's wishes are honored. These meetings are often like a boat without a rudder and takes patience to regain direction. Remember, *listening* will begin to set you on the right course. The ideas and content of this section also applies to couples and families.

As an individual you can answer the questions and/or ask your own. Some people use techniques of asking themselves a burning question and stay with it until a clear response begins to emerge. This can be done in silent contemplation, writing, visual art, or whatever works for you to connect with yourself and "look within to see."

When I use this process I'm often surprised when an answer comes after I let go of trying too hard to find it. The writing and/or contemplation or however you begin can reveal what you didn't know you knew. After all, somewhere within each of us we know everything we need to know. Focusing on the question or subject is like having a fishing pole dipped into a deep pond of knowing. The living proof of that for me has been writing this book and guide. Writing was the fishing pole that became a way to look within and find what wants to be said. In this way I've come to trust writing can cause contemplation that goes far deeper than I knew was possible.

What Groups Have Done and Suggestions
Groups created the following ideas, content and activities to deepen their connection. With this intention every thing you do actually fulfills the purpose of deepening including the heart storming sessions.

Some Groups Changed The Following:
    1. Meet twice a month.
    2. Meet outside of the meetings more often.

3. Change the format to engage with members after check-in. This interaction is given decided upon time to leave space for the topic of the day.
4. Group discussion after each member responds to the topic or activity.
5. I recommend facilitation for meetings that have a theme.

List of Questions Developed by Members
Some groups continued with responses to questions created by the members. Some earlier topics spark questions for deeper inquiry. How to investigate these topics becomes a heart storming session. This lasted until other interests were offered for group decision

1. How has preparing for death and dying deepened our connection as a group?
2. What else do we need to deepen our preparation for death and dying?
3. What did we learn from our mothers and fathers about living and dying?
4. Let's talk about our fathers and what we learned about men, women and relationships. What did we learn about ourselves as women?
5. Let's share about the process of our experience with aging, the losses and gains along the way.
6. How have we done so far in relinquishing old roles and identities?
7. Let's share about how we were as little girls and how we are today. What have we learned and what has changed since our days of innocence?
8. Religious and spiritual journeys we would like to share with the group.
9. Let's share about our bodies, our sexuality and our health at this time of our lives.
10. How identified and attached are we to our physical forms?

11. How do we feel about being or not being grandparents? What is our relationship with our grand kids? How do we relate to our children as parents?
12. What is our legacy and what we will leave behind for the world? What mark have we made or still hope to make before we leave this world?
13. Other content and activities that let's us know more about each other. Have a day of shared photos as children, our parents and grand parents, weddings and other important times in our lives.

How we feel about our later years:

1. What beliefs do you have about aging? Are they true in your experience?
2. Do you think elder wisdom is valued in our culture? Does this affect you?
3. What makes some people seem ageless?
4. What qualities make an enjoyable life in our later years?
5. What do you value most about your life right now? What gives you the most happiness and fulfillment?
6. What is most difficult for you at this stage of life? What gifts have come from your time of aging?
7. Do you have any other words of wisdom to share with the circle?

Books to Share and Discuss
The following books were read by at least one member and introduced to the group to be read and discussed. To take it deeper each person shares how the content of the book is relative to them and how a part affected their way of living. Books to read are decided by the group.

The Grace in Dying, How We Are Transformed Spiritually As We Die by Kathleen
Dowling Singh.

This book offers a profound perception about the experience of dying. The content inspires reflection. Members can offer ways to approach the book and form questions that may follow. The book follows the teachings of the Buddha as a background for the experience of transformation. However, in my times of being with the dying transformation does happen both in the person dying as well as with others involved. This is a deeply felt look into an experience not usually written about due to the emotions and the mystery surrounding the dying process. This book can open your heart and give you peace of mind about death and dying.

The Untethered Soul by Michael A. Singer
One group read a chapter before each meeting and discussed how the messages and suggestions affected their lives. One member asked the group, "What are you tethered to in your life?"

Living Deeply, The Art & Science of Transformation in Everyday Life. This is based on a research program at the Institute of Noetic Sciences. The book contains wisdom from Ram Das, Stanislav Grof, Angeles Arrien, Jon Kabat-Zinn and many others.

Group Processes
The following are processes agreed upon by the group. A member could have experienced the process. However, the processes can be done if one or more members avail themselves of online information, use workbooks or take a workshop on the subject.

I recommend both *The Work* by Byron Katie and NVC (Non Violent Communication). Both are excellent practices for groups, couples, parents, grandparents and all relationships. These teachings will enhance your way of relating and communicating with skills not usually taught in our educational system.
Google: The Work of Byron Katie www.thework.com
Non-violent Communication
www.nonviolentcommunication.com

The Work by Byron Katie can give us a look under the covers to see how we really think and believe. This opportunity to know ourselves gives us more options to meet life more skillfully and with more kindness.

The process offered in *The Work* can be revisited often. Once again we look at our beliefs and how they affect our relationships and our way of seeing life. We often don't realize we have a point of view, a way of thinking or handling our lives until we become more aware of how we respond or react to various situations.

The section on Deepening Our Connection is the perfect arena for practicing Nonviolent Communication. NVC, developed by Marshall Rosenberg, is really showing respect for people in the form of communication. Since most of us didn't grow up with this way of speaking to each other, NVC has a practice workbook. Practicing in the group creates a safe place for members to communicate clearly with more compassion.

Nonviolent communication was a life changer for me. I never knew my communications often carried hidden critical innuendoes until I saw them in the light of NVC. Learning the difference between a request and a demand was a revelation. Asking a person if they are willing to do something and really meaning it as a request allows the person to respond without feeling obligated. I began to share my feelings without making anyone wrong. This made it possible for people to hear my communication rather than putting up a wall of protection.

Processes Offered by Group Members
There are many life enhancing processes, activities, books and group experiences we haven't thought of yet to deepen our connection. Members can offer processes they have learned then used in their own lives. I recommend a short talk to share the purpose with the members. A demonstration of the practice is beneficial. Or the group can trust and see what happens and what can be learned. Be sure to give feedback and reflections about your experience. Both positive and well-meaning feedback offers support and builds confidence in those sharing the process.

Experiences and processes created by members are often tuned to the needs of the group. Members know what appeals to the group and what can be done to take members deeper in their lives and their relationship with each other. Remember, this is a proving ground to find ways to deepen our connection and form a family of friends for life. Whatever you do will accomplish this beautiful need if given focus and commitment. You can do no wrong for everything is a learning process. We are learning to pick up the stitches we dropped along the way and begin to weave trust and caring into the tapestry of our lives.

Group Ideas and Experiences:

- Two or three members come together and create a process for the group. Often these exercises originate from experiences in life and are offered as a group activity. This gives everyone a chance to have fun "heart storming" and co-creating a meeting.

- Some groups occasionally use nonverbal ways of communicating such as dance or movement. Nonverbal expression used at check-in and the gratitude circle is also a creative change.

- At times several members take turns reading their favorite poetry while other members move to the rhythms and visuals in the poetry. You may want to read the poem while half the group moves while the other half observes. Then change places. What the poem conveys is embodied as the movement takes place and becomes an even deeper experience of the poem and it's meaning.

- Story Telling can take many directions. The group can choose one theme or each member chooses one that appeals to them. Telling stories about ourselves lets others know how we relate to life and the world. This exercise can go on for several meetings. I recommend agreeing on how much time each person has to share their story.

Tell a story:
- o from your childhood that formed who you are to this day
- o that was a turning point in your life
- o about a time you felt really afraid
- o about discovering your courage
- o about rescue. Yours or one you preformed
- o you would only tell your closest friends
- o that revealed something you didn't know about yourself
- o that opened your heart
- o about a deeply experienced connection

Stay in touch via emails, phone, birthdays or any way you create with other members. Members often send each other uplifting information and health gems from the internet.
- Expressing in visual art, movement, song, poetry, prose, comedy

- Group meditation

- One day or more group vacations

- Overnight sleep-over

- Learn something new *together* such as playing the harp, singing, collage making, dancing, acting, water aerobics, computer graphics, card making, healthy gourmet cooking and so many others you've always wanted to learn. In this way you can have fun taking classes together and continue encouraging and learning from each other.

- Let your creativity soar, your heart expand and by all means enjoy every moment of deepening in every way.

- Some groups revisit *A Year to Live*. After several years of deepening it will be like "arriving at the same place and know it for the first time." Also revisit One More Day to give each other gratitude in a special way.

As the poem by one of our Angels, Judith Small, expresses so beautifully,
"Let the years pass slowly slow, for there is so much more of you I wish to know."

Bon voyage, my friends enjoy yourselves with your friends for life.

PART EIGHT

GUIDELINES FOR FACILITATORS

"Intuition is a sacred gift, the rational mind is a
faithful servant."
Albert Einstein

When you consciously use both, facilitation becomes
a way of life.
Darrienne

Introduction

The Angel 'Ohana is a dynamic group with multidimensional experiences. The guide is structured, along with facilitation, for this multi-layered experience to fulfill its purpose. Of course, at times you will be called upon to play everything by heart and use your intuition to manage a circle of diverse humans expressing themselves. With the format and guidelines in place you can bring the group back to the central purpose from its natural tangents.

The Angel Ohana *is not* a therapy group or a place to process relationships that take place in or outside of the group. If you need to communicate regarding an upset, do so outside of the meetings. The meetings are a place to build deep bonds of friendship that take time and patience. We are creating a safe place to share what's most important to each of us, look into the deeper questions of life and in the process become guides and teachers for each other.

At times and in some groups a few people will drop out. If they speak to you before the next meeting, ask them to come and say their farewell. If they choose not to come announce it in the group and say why the person or persons left the group. If a person is leaving for some time and wants to remain in the group, ask the group if they would be open to the individual returning.

Often members want to add new members when they understand the purpose of the Angel 'Ohana from personal experience. Earlier additions are best. However, new people can come in during the section on The Later Years and before Embracing Our Mortality. New additions need to be agreed upon by the group. The member introducing the new person is responsible for catch up. The member will also accompany the new person in filling out The Five Wishes and The Angel Ohana Personal Profile. Make sure the new member understands the Angel Buddy and Advocate system.

Choosing to Facilitate
The word "facilitate" means to make easy/easier, forward, encourage, to make possible. A facilitator listens in order to sense how to support the collective agreed upon intention of the members. It could be the general theme or topic of the day as well as the general purpose of connecting and support. She listens to each member's needs and implements what works for the group as a whole. She does not have to make decisions because she asks the group for feedback and facilitates finding a collective agreement. This supports group participation.

The choice to facilitate a group is an opportunity to learn about yourself and others. You are actually in a relationship with the whole group. You may bump into all those little things in yourself that have wanted attention all your life. This is the blessing of all relationships even though at the time it may not seem that way. I suggest the facilitator choose one or two people in the group to be a support team to meet with her outside of the meetings. The job of the team is to listen to her feelings and talk over how to proceed when necessary.

Relationships are great mirrors that reflect both ways. Just knowing this gives you a heads up, making it easier to simply observe what's happening without judging yourself or anyone else. Becoming a facilitator of a group is like having a constant trainer for listening deeper than the words. Body language can tell you how the person feels even if the words seem to convey something different. This isn't for comment or discussion in the group. What the body says gives the facilitator information about how to proceed or give more time to the member to express feelings.

I encourage each member to take a turn facilitating. Holding the space for the purpose to unfold deepens your relationship to each member and to the group as a whole. This experience gives you an overview of group interaction. You will be able to observe how the group affects each member and how each member affects the group. In this way you can support the group toward building trust and wanting the best for each other. When you are no longer facilitating, this awareness and support remains.

Three to six months is usual for the role of facilitator. For those of you who are not facilitating, please give the facilitator your support and gratitude. Only give feedback when asked. No group or meeting is ever the same. Remember, facilitation is on-job-training for everyone, even for those with years of experience.

Facilitating The Angel 'Ohana Group

As a facilitator the first thing to know is you wear two hats. You will be facilitating the group as well as being a member of the group. Remember, The Angel Ohana is built on the premise there is no one teacher and we are all teaches for each other. You may become a teacher like anyone in the circle when it's your time to check-in or when you respond to questions in the topics.

Choosing A Contact Person

A person to stay in touch with the members by email or phone is an essential part of the group. Ask for a volunteer at the first meeting. The contact person sends out emails a week before the next meeting as a reminder of the topic and the location. When there are changes or the meeting is canceled, she contacts the members. The contact person can also assist the facilitator in making decisions and discuss ideas to further support the group. It's a good idea to have a person that supports the facilitator.

What's Most Important

As stated in the Introduction, engaging in meaningful conversation holds the key to happiness for two main reasons: because humans are inspired to find and create meaning in their lives, and because we are social animals that need to connect.

With this in mind, regardless of the content of the meeting, *what is most important* is what is actually taking place with each member and/or with the group as a whole. Give this your attention. You may want to comment on what's happening for clarification or to heighten awareness.

If a member needs attention give them time to express themselves. Ask the member if they have a need and a request for that need. Remember a request is only a *request* and lets others know what is needed. This is not a demand of fulfillment. If it's not clear what to do, ask the group how they would like to proceed. When things feel complete, you can always go back to the planned topic of the day. If time is short ask members if they would like to stay a few more minutes or continue at the next meeting.

Building a Safe Environment

The format and the themes are designed to build safety and create bonds of trust among members as well as with the group as a whole.

The facilitator is the caretaker of the group. She begins by establishing a safe and welcoming environment. Focused listening in the group offers the feeling of being heard and develops confidence in each other. Equality of sharing time and attention lets members know each person is important. Safety allows vulnerability and the strength to express ones own truth. When we know we are in safe hands, friendship goes beyond casual or guarded acquaintances.

Often members want to add new members when they understand the purpose of the Angel 'Ohana from personal experience. Earlier additions are best. However, new people can come in during the section on The Later Years and before Embracing Our Mortality. New additions need to be agreed upon by the group. The member introducing the new person is responsible for catch up. The member will also accompany the new person in filling out The Five Wishes and The Angel Ohana Personal Profile. Make sure the new member understands the Angel Buddy and Advocate system.

At times and in some groups a few people will drop out. If they speak to you before the next meeting, ask them to come and say their farewell. If they choose not to come announce it in the group and say why the person or persons left the group. If a person is leaving for some time and wants to remain in the group, ask the group if they would be open to the individual returning.

The Sacred Circle
It is vital that members honor, "What is shared in the circle, stays in the circle." Be sure to discuss and gain agreement.

Keeping the sanctity of the sharing circle is key to building trust and dependability. This simply means that each person is revered for who they are and what they share is worthy of being heard and kept within the circle. It is the responsibility of the facilitator and each member to protect this agreement.

Content and Process
There is a difference between the content of themes and the process taking place in the group. Individuals are interested in content and what it has to do with them. As a facilitator you are

aware of the process of how members respond to each other, how they respond to the theme and questions and participate in the group. When you see the "big picture" you become aware of the how the group as a whole is moving toward the guiding purpose of bonding and support.

Group interaction can be fascinating. The process of individuals becoming a functioning group of caring members takes time and intention. The willingness for individuals to become part of a group and feel connected to the group with affection is key to building trust. This is when a sense of family begins to take place. Members begin to know they are all on this journey together and want the best for each other. Being able to see this coming about can give the facilitator the advantage of supporting the process.

Then there is the "personality" of the group itself. Is the group mostly open and cooperative or do some members wait for others to make things work? Some members can jump right in and bond as a group right away. Some groups want to meet more often and plan things to do together between the regular meetings. Others take longer to feel safe in a "family" or community environment. Most of us have had little experience in a family that actually works or a community with close bonds of lasting friendships. As the facilitator you are the reminder of the patience needed to create something new with the intention of engaging in a life of kinship. When you are watching the group as a whole you will begin to see members moving towards the purpose of deepening their connection with each other. As the facilitator you can share what you see in order to bring more awareness to the group's direction or what could be holding it back. Do this by sharing your own feelings without pointing out any person or several members. Describe what you observe and how you feel without judgmental comments.

Examples of Attending to Process

After check-in begin the topic for the day. When members talk about problems or issues unrelated to the general theme, the group can go off focus. In this case, remind the group, "We've gone of focus." Ask the group, "Would you like to go back to the topic?"

Most will say they want to stay with the topic. If not, find out what is needed at the moment. It's best to use a "talking item" for these discussions so that everyone has a chance to express themselves. You may ask for another round so members can offer solutions.

After everyone has spoken, including yourself, you can say how you feel about the way things are going. This is your viewpoint and it is often beneficial because you usually see the bigger picture. You have your finger on the pulse of the group as a whole and can sense where it wants to go. Or you might say, "I'm not sure where we want to go next. Are there any suggestions from the group?" This includes the group in the decision making process.

Often these interests or concerns become the topic for the next meeting. Ask the group for an agreement to change the focus for one meeting. Let the group know the following meeting will be the next topic in the guide.

Allowing attention to emerge related to building trust and connection keeps the group alive and develops creative interaction. However, staying with general themes and topics gives structure and safety and a sense of common direction. Each situation tells you how to proceed. Coming back to the topics in the guide gives the group a feeling of continuity.

Group Challenges and Ways They Can Be Met

- At times someone leaves the group for reason such as illness, relocating to another area, or death. Regardless of the reason there are always feelings of loss and a sense the person is still part of the group.

- Often we have a ceremony to say goodbye after the person has left the group. An alter can be made in the center of the circle perhaps with flowers, a crystal or group photo. Each person lights a candle in turn and says how they feel about the person and say their personal goodbye.

- One of the groups had a challenge with members coming and going on trips. They also had several members move away or drop out for various reasons. This had an affect on the members and how they felt about building trust and long-term relationships.

- You can send a group email to say: "There has been a feeling of inconsistency in the group caused by members going on trips, or not coming to some meetings. I know this has an affect on me. How has this affected you?" This will be the subject of the next meeting. (Voice your feelings in the sharing circle.) Let's talk about commitment and what that means to you. This is also a good time for members to restate their purpose as a member of the Angel 'Ohana. You may want to ask again what they want to receive and what they want to give.

Although each meeting is set up with specific directions for the day they are only guidelines to help the group stay on focus. Using the structure of the format (no advice, analysis or comments unless asked for by the member) creates safety for each person to share. The directions are suggestion not hard lines to follow. So, follow the directions for sharing and stay with the format when you can.

Example: If someone is in physical or emotional pain at the moment of sharing or anytime in the group you can say, "We would like to sit with you in silence for awhile." After a few minutes she may pass the "Talking Item" on to the next person. If she passes the item on or if she does not, you can say, "We are here for you. How we can support you right now? What is your request?" Take time for a request to form and for the group to find a way to respond. (Use your own words to convey the essence of this intention.)

Practice
    Being a facilitator takes practice. It's also a practice for life. Being awake to the present moment from a place of awareness gives life another dimension. You have stepped back and observed the event without getting entangled in emotions or thoughts. This observation can include noticing your own experience of what's taking place. This benefits facilitation as well as a freer way of attending to a situation as it is at the moment. Giving attention

to the group as a whole without burying your own personal needs and feelings is great practice for CEOs, teachers, parents and political leaders.

Awareness also includes the comfort of the members, the heat or coolness and the lighting in the room. It's also means tuning into what's happening in the circle as if it were an entity itself. By "tuning in" I mean seeing and feeling the general tone of the circle that day. Check-in time may give you a clue. During check-in a member may need more time to share. She may want to bring her experience into the circle by asking a question. If the member needs support ask, "How can we support you? What is your need and a request that can fulfill the need?"

The "how" to support and meet the request may take time to investigate or resolve.

Facilitating the Angel 'Ohana Meetings

A reminder of the topic and location of the meeting is emailed to members one week before the meeting. If someone doesn't have email, the contact person calls the member as a reminder of the topic and time and place to meet.

Since members will have the guide they will be able to read the topic and questions before the next meeting. If the topic has been changed the contact person sends a reminder of the alternate topic. In the last section, Deepening Our Connection, there will be many topics that are not in the guide. These topics and activities need reminders a week before the meeting.

The Meeting Format

Welcome and Thanks
Begin each meeting by welcoming the group. Also thank the person hosting the meeting. I ask for information about the house, location of the restroom, water or tea, etc.
Silent Time

Begin each meeting with ten minutes of silence. Ring a bell to begin and again when the silent time is over. Silence is a great way to relax and brings the group together in resonance.

Start on time. This gives the group a sense of continuity and dependability that contributes to feeling safe.

After Silent Time state the format of the meeting and topic of the day. This is important for members to know what the day looks like so they can relax.

Check-in:
Remind the group what's shared in the circle stays in the circle. Check-in lets the group know how members are at the moment. By sharing what is most important members learn about the person and can learn from their experience.

I have been asked how to keep the sharing on point without some members talking a long time or getting lost in stories of the past. The format keeps the circle alive when members express what's present for them at the time of sharing.

I also remind the group we can only give our undivided attention for short periods of time, usually about 90 to 120 seconds. After that our minds tend to wander. You may need to remind the group for several meetings *before* check-in begins.

Sharing in The Meetings
The facilitator opens the sharing with the following reminders until they become natural to the group.
- Please keep the sharing brief so that each member has a chance to speak.
- Stay with the response to the question without irrelevant comments. Staying in the moment often helps to keep the response alive on point of what is being asked.
- You can usually say what's most important in the first few minutes of sharing. After that we tend to explain ourselves, repeat what was said or get lost from the original subject.
- The "talking item" is a reminder to share from the heart. You can hold it without speaking until the connection is felt. Pass the item to the next person if nothing is there to

share at the moment. (Facilitator lets the person know she will come back after everyone has a turn.)
- At times a member needs a few moments of silence to look inside and form words to communicate what they would like to express.
- Some groups decide to have a time-keeper. The time-keeper rings a bell or her timer makes a sound when the decided upon time for sharing is done. The time for check in or sharing can be structured by the number of people in the group.

The person sharing can take time to finish the thought. If sharing goes on too
long the time keeper rings the bell again or gives a signal of 'times up'.

Break Times:
After check-in is a good time to ask the group to stand up and shake out the sitting. A way to wake up the body is to stand up in a circle, turn to the right and rub the person's shoulder in front of you. Start out softly and when you hear "oohs" and 'ahs" you can rub a bit deeper. Then turn to the left and start over with another person. Ask a member to offer a different exercise after check-in for the next meeting.
Some groups take a short five-minute break for "tea and pee". Longer than that you can lose the focus. Others groups prefer not to interrupt the flow. Members get up and quietly take care of what they need to do.
At times ask the group to stand up and give each other a hug when something moving happens. Often this turns into a group hug.

Topics for The Meetings:
After check-in, the facilitator gives a brief summery of the topic for the day. Before each round of sharing repeat the questions in the guide.
- The facilitator introduces the topic. In order to set the tone for the meeting you can read the introduction for the topic from the guide. Add what you'd like to say in your

own words. If you like, read a poem or quote appropriate to the theme.

- Ask the first question and pass the talking item. If no one responds then the facilitator goes first. This often opens the way for the sharing to begin.
- If there are two questions state the second question and pass the talking item around again.
- If there isn't a second question ask if anyone has more to say or has a question for the group. This is also a good time for members to ask each other to say more or ask a question for clarification about what was shared.
- If there are more than two questions, read them all and ask members to choose which one or ones apply or stir a response.
- If there is time, open the circle to conversation.
- You can sum up the sharing. Comment on the interest in the topic and the energy of the group. If you sense there is more to be done ask the group if they would like to continue the topic at the next meeting.

Gratitude Circle
End the meeting with a gratitude circle. It's important for the group to end on a good note. Stand in a circle and allow time for members to "feel" their gratitude before they speak. Some groups spontaneously hold hands and give a little squeeze when done or Om or give yelps of joy.

Logistics
Ask a volunteer to host the next meeting. Some meetings take place at the same location. Ask for other concerns, changes and decisions to be made.
State the topic for the next meeting.

The Circle has come to a close. You've done a good job!

Special Situations You May Encounter

- For the first meetings it's helpful to have the same facilitator until the group settles in. This could be the person who organized the group or someone who would like to facilitate. After members begin to feel comfortable with each other and the format, the facilitation can be passed on. I recommend the person read Guidelines for Facilitators even if they have had previous experience with groups.

- There will come a time in all circles when the facilitator has to wing it and play it by heart. This means to sense the group feeling and navigate by what is calling for attention. Knowing your overall purpose is to support the group's intention to bond and honor each member's well-being will guide you.

- A member's mother died and we gave her time as needed to share her experience and feelings. Her sharing turned into a blessing for the group. Those of us whose mothers had died also shared our experience. This was a special sharing for everyone.

- A member told the group she felt very depressed and didn't want to come to the meeting. I asked if she would be willing to come into the center of the circle so the group could be with her.
  o I asked if she would be willing for us to come around her and put our hands on her body. When she agreed we gently placed our hands in silence.
  o Someone began to hum and we all made soft sounds together. Then we asked, "Will you let us know if you feels the way again?." She said, "Yes".
  o After this encouragement she attended every meeting. Everyone knew we could count on each

other when we need reminding our dark times don't have to be faced alone.

- There will be other times you need to let go of the format of the meeting. It is always beneficial to the whole circle to take care of situations as they occur. For example: Please remind a member that forgets that the sharing is sacred and interruptions can interfere with a person's focus.

- Example: If a member is upset with the group or it's process and wants to bring it to the group this can be stated after the silent time. Offer the member the talking item first so they can share the origin of the upset. Pass the item for other members to respond. There may be several rounds of sharing and may take the whole meeting. At the end of the sharing and responses, ask the member if her upset is resolved. While these meetings may seem divisive they often end in sharing our truth that becomes a bonding opportunity. In a well-functioning family, every one's point of view is respected and given time to be shared and heard.

- If someone is a constant drain on group energy it is a different situation. Communicate with the person by describing the situation without being critical. Do this outside of the meeting. Say how you feel and ask if the person would be willing to respond to what is being said. This could open a free and compassionate conversation about the person's needs and the needs of the group. The person may realize the group doesn't meet her needs and she may want to be in another kind of group. This rarely happens because the purpose of the Angel 'Ohana is made very clear. If the situation persists, the group must decide how to take care of this distraction from bonding and support.

Other Guidelines for Facilitating the Group:

- Start the meeting at the agreed upon time even if everyone is not there. Welcome anyone who is late when they come into the circle (unless it's during the silent time). At the end of meeting ask everyone to be on time if possible. Being on time let's members know you care enough to begin together.
- After the silent time, state the format of the meeting: check-in, topic of the day, gratitude circle and logistics. When the group gets a sense of the usual format this part can be dropped except stating the topic of the day. If the usual format is different that day give a summery of the meeting and what was accomplished.

- If a person isn't ready to share remind them to pass the talking item on to the next person and it will come back when everyone has spoken.

- Remind the group each person's sharing is a time to be honored and respected. This gives members time to contemplate their response and find words for expression. No questions are asked or feedback or advice is given during each sharing. If the person sharing asks for feedback, this can be given after the meeting. Protecting the sharing time of each person is important in order to create a safe space.

- Some groups with ten or more people ask for a volunteer to be a timer. I suggest the time for check-in be no more than two to three minutes. Response to the topic and questions may take more time. The group can decide the time in relationship to the number of members. The person timing softly rings a bell when time is up. The person sharing can finish the sentence. The bell rings again if the person continues. The person timing or the facilitator reminds the group how much time is left to complete the sharing.

This is a delicate situation and needs group feedback as how to proceed with the sharing time.

- Stay tuned to the energy of the group in order to know if a break is needed.

- There are usually 2 or 3 questions to begin the response to the topic of that day.

After the first round of sharing the next round can be an open discussion. Often an open round of sharing regarding the topic is necessary due to ideas, feelings and questions that have come out of the first one or two rounds. After response to the questions I ask the group if they want an open conversation about the theme of the day. Let members know how much time there is for discussion.

Make sure to keep the last ten or fifteen minutes of the meeting for The Gratitude Circle. This time is essential for ending the day with gratitude and warm feelings about each other.

- At the end of the meeting make a date and place for the next meeting. If a specific topic comes out of the sharing that is not in The Guide, ask if everyone agrees to this topic for the next meeting. If there is not unanimous agreement, go to back to the guide. The new topic can be addressed at another time.

- At the end of each theme let everyone know we are entering a new theme for the next meeting. I begin with The Later Years. At the end of that theme I ask the group if they would like to go further or go to The Five Wishes and Embracing Our Mortality. The benefit of the group making decisions and choosing directions offers an opportunity for other inquiries to be heard and creates an arena for new ideas to be considered.

The Healing Circle When someone isn't feeling well, is sad or in grief or is recuperating from illness, ask the group to form a Healing Circle *before* the Gratitude Circle. Ask the person if they would like to stand in the center of the circle. Ask if any one else would like to stand in the circle. The group gathers around the person or persons and uses the sound of Om or hums or sings a healing song. The whole circle often forms a group hug. Just follow your heart.

I commend you for the courage to strengthen your great heart. Being a facilitator can do this and more than I can say. Each person will find their own lessons and from that you will learn about yourself and others. Discovering how groups become a family of the heart is a priceless education.

EPILOGUE

This book has been my constant companion and valiant teacher as I entered my later years. In my wildest dreams I never thought I'd write a book. In the beginning, writing down my wobbly thoughts taught me (and finally you) what the wisdom years, deepening our connection and The Angel 'Ohana are about. It's here on these pages the purpose was born and the depths of all three led me to writing. Until I could see the authenticity of *deepening our connection* was being realized in The Angel 'Ohana I couldn't stop. Thoughts may still be wobbly until the words come to match what wants to be said and there is always more that wants to happen. The 'more' is a legacy for you and all the Angels of future 'ohanas.

I only ask you to use 'the guide' as the guide it's meant to be. For humans are varied in their way of life and all want to love and be loved without conditions. Just trust your heart and support members being true to themselves. The Angel 'Ohana is a true 'ohana in the making. There is no right or wrong way to do it. A steady hand and an open mind are your best allies to make the mistakes that are compost for new beginnings. Of course an open heart goes unsaid for without that you would not be reading this at all. Because you *are* reading, there is nothing more to say except, "Mahalo* for joining me in this adventure. And Arigato* because life is too difficult to live alone...I'm grateful for your presence and love you just as you are and always have been."

*Mahalo, "Thank you" in Hawaiian language.
*Arigato is often used in Japanese to say "Thank you." The deeper meaning is "Life is too difficult to live alone. I'm grateful for your presence."

Made in the USA
San Bernardino, CA
23 November 2013